Hamlyn nature guides

Fossils

Hamlyn nature guides

Fossils

Richard Moody

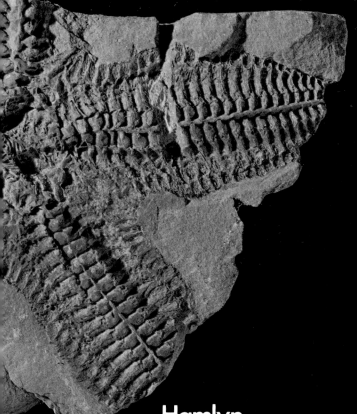

Hamlyn
London · New York · Sydney · Toronto

Acknowledgements

The following are N.E.R.C. Copyright, reproduced by permission of the Director, Institute of Geological Sciences, London S.W.7.: title spread, 36L, 41L, 41R, 42R, 48R, 54L, 66L, 76L, 99R, 103L, 105L, 107L, 109R, 122R.
Ardea – P. J. Green 123L; Biofotos back cover, 33R, 93L; Hervé Chaumeton front cover, 17R, 38R, 63R, 68R, 73R, 79L, 80L, 80R, 81L, 83L, 84L, 89R, 91L, 94R, 95R, 120L, 122L; Adrian Davies 65L, 69L, 72R, 86R, 112R, 133R, 125L; Hamlyn Group Picture Library 18L, 34L, 50L, 93R, 98R, 99L, 100R, 116L; Hunterian Museum 30L, 60L, 60R, 74R, 83R, 84R, 86L, 88R, 89L, 90L, 95L, 96L, 101L, 104R, 106R, 110L, 112L; Oxford Scientific Film Unit – W. J. Kennedy 20L, 29L, 29R, 50R, 78L, 78R, 81L, 82L, 102L, 108R, 110R; J. C. Revy 79R, 119R, 123R; R.I.D.A. Photo Library – R. T. J. Moody 26R, 35R, 57L, 70R, 109L, 111R, 124R; R.I.D.A. Photo Library – David Bayliss 14R, 15L, 15R, 16L, 16R, 18R, 19L, 19R, 20R, 21R, 22L, 22R, 23L, 23R, 24L, 24R, 25L, 25R, 26L, 26R, 27L, 27R, 28L, 28R, 30R, 31L, 31R, 32L, 32R, 34R, 36R, 37L, 37R, 38L, 39L, 39R, 40L, 40R, 42L, 42R, 43L, 43R, 44L, 44R, 45L, 45R, 46L, 46R, 47R, 48L, 49R, 51L, 51R, 52L, 52R, 53L, 53R, 54R, 55L, 55R, 56L, 56R, 57R, 58L, 58R, 59R, 61L, 61R, 62L, 62R, 63L, 64R, 65R, 66R, 67L, 67R, 68L, 69R, 70L, 71L, 71R, 72L, 73L, 75L, 75R, 76R, 77L, 77R, 81R, 82R, 85R, 87L, 87R, 88L, 90R, 91R, 92L, 92R, 96R, 97L, 97R, 98L, 100L, 101R, 103L, 103R, 105R, 106L, 107R, 108L, 110L, 113L, 114L, 114R, 115L, 115R, 116R, 117R, 118L, 118R, 119L, 120R, 121R, 124L, 125R; David J. Siveter 102R.

To my mother

The author wishes to thank Miss S. Cornish, Mrs F. Mouton, Dr J. S. Penn, Mrs S. Pickering, Mr G. Raine and Dr D. Wright for their help in the preparation and presentation of this book; and the trustees of the British Museum (Natural History) and Kingston Polytechnic for allowing their specimens to be photographed.

Line drawings by Linda Parry

Published by The Hamlyn Publishing Group Limited
London. New York. Sydney. Toronto
Astronaut House, Feltham, Middlesex, England
Copyright © The Hamlyn Publishing Group Limited 1979

ISBN 0 600 33654 9

Phototypeset by Tradespools Limited
Frome, Somerset

Printed in Italy

Contents

Introduction

Since life began on Earth over 3000 million years ago the remains and traces of plants and animals have been preserved in rocks deposited both on land and in the sea. These remains and traces were known to scholars such as Xenophanes and Herodotus long before the birth of Christ. The Latin words **fossilia petrificata** were used in the description of petrified organisms from the earth's surface, but now, the word 'fossil' is applied to the remains of organisms preserved throughout geological time. Ancient scholars knew little of geology or evolution, and the scientific study of fossils is relatively recent.

A fossil may represent the almost complete remains of an animal or plant. However, this is very rare and the majority of fossils usually feature only the more durable parts of an organism. In animals this refers to the shells, tests, and skeletons of creatures without backbones and the bones of vertebrates. Plants are mainly represented by the fossilization of woody tissues, but seeds and leaves are common in younger rocks. Fossils may also take the form of moulds or casts which reflect either the internal or external character of the animal. The term 'body fossil' is applied to the remains of the actual organism, the original chemical composition of which may change with the passage of time. Some processes, described

millions of years	period	epoch	
— 2·5	Quaternary	Recent	Cainozoic
		Pleistocene	
	Tertiary	Pliocene	
		Miocene	
		Oligocene	
		Eocene	
— 65		Palaeocene	
	Cretaceous		Mesozoic
— 136	Jurassic		
— 190	Triassic		
— 225	Permian		
— 280	Upper Carboniferous		Palaeozoic
— 325	Lower Carboniferous		
— 345	Devonian		
— 395	Silurian		
— 430	Ordovician		
— 500	Cambrian		
— 570	Pre-Cambrian		

The geological time-scale.

more fully below, may actually enhance the beauty of the specimen but others may ultimately destroy the evidence of past life. Trace fossils — the tracks, trails, and burrows which reflect the habits and movements of animals — seldom suffer from the action of chemical activity; the cementing of sediments preserving forever the record of past activities.

The vast majority of fossils represent animals and plants that lived in aquatic environments such as lakes, rivers, or seas. Land animals and plants are rarely

Trace fossils are very useful for the recognition of environments throughout the stratigraphic column, and their complexity often reflects the feeding habits of the animal involved in their construction.

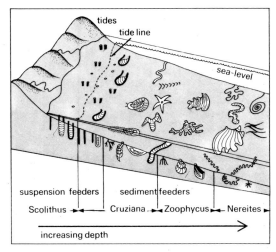

The relationships of flora and fauna to their aquatic habitats. A, the basic subdivisions of both marine and terrestrial environments; B, the distribution of algae and invertebrate animals (both past and present) in aquatic environments.

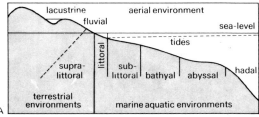

preserved in situ because the agents of weathering, scavengers, and bacterial action quickly destroy and scatter their remains. Organisms that die in water, however, are often buried rapidly by the deposition of muds or sands; these sediments protect the specimen from the adverse factors noted above. Infrequently, the conditions that prevail are such that the finest details of both soft and hard parts are preserved. Collections from the Burgess Shales of Canada (Middle Cambrian) and the Lithographic Limestone of Bavaria (Upper Jurassic) contain many beautiful almost complete fossils and impressions of extinct organisms.

The original shell materials of animals may be preserved in the fossil record; but it is only to be expected that the further one goes back in geological time, the more likely it is, that the composition of the shell has been subject to change. The mode of preservation of an organism tells us much about its

This reconstruction illustrates the various niches and habitats occupied by animals in the marine environment. Through detailed collection and analysis palaeontologists are often able to reconstruct such models for ancient faunas.

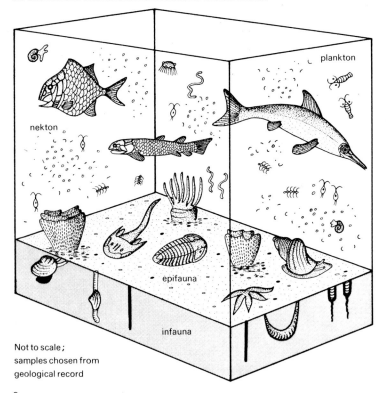

plankton

nekton

epifauna

infauna

Not to scale; samples chosen from geological record

history since death, and is often correlated with the type of sediment in which the fossil is found. Unaltered hard parts such as the bones of Cainozoic mammals or the aragonitic shells of Tertiary molluscs are common to many parts of the world; but the majority of Mesozoic and Palaeozoic organisms exhibit some degree of alteration. In plants, arthropods, graptolites, and fish this alteration may take the form of a reduction of the volatile chemical constituents; a thin carbon film replacing the original materials. This reduction process is termed **carbonization**. Where shells and bones have a porous nature the deposition of minerals from the surrounding sediments may infill the spaces. The process is one of impregnation, the fossils becoming harder and heavier in character. The term applied to this type of alteration is **petrification**.

In some fossils such as brachiopods or bivalves the original shell structure may be altered by solution and reprecipitation. The original fibrous or layered structure is destroyed and a crystal mosaic is deposited in its place. **Recrystallization**, as this process is termed, may be very fine or coarse in character. When the original material of the shell is dissolved away, the space left may be occupied by other minerals such as silica or iron pyrites, and **replacement** is said to have taken place. If minerals do not occupy the vacated area of shell materials, then the palaeontologist can only rely on the **moulds** and **casts** left within the enclosing sediment for information.

The idea of a field guide, like the *Treatise on Invertebrate Paleontology*, is to help the collector identify individual specimens. While the details of preservation may help in the interpretation of modes of life which are essentially based on field and laboratory observations, a guide, in itself, is a practical aid. However, reference to original descriptive works must be undertaken if the correct **generic** and **specific** names are to be allocated. These constitute the scientific name given to a particular specimen; identical individuals together form a **species** and numbers of species may be included in one **genus**. The name is binomial, for example, *Equus asinus* is the name given to the ass.

Collecting fossils

In recent years, the study of geology at all levels has undergone a dramatic increase and the collection of rocks, minerals, and fossils has become a major hobby. Most collectors are responsible people but some, often motivated by financial gain, do great harm to both the subject and to the localities from which they collect. Land owners, quarry managers, and local councils are often very helpful to both amateur and professional geologist but, like any guardian, rightly frown on any careless or wanton behaviour. Anyone who purchases a guide related to the identification of fossils or minerals is obviously interested in collecting original specimens and therefore, if the opportunities for future field work are to be preserved, they will be keen to observe the 'code of conduct' initiated by the Geologists' Association, London. This code is not intended to deter interest but it is an attempt to relieve the collecting pressure on the limited number of irreplaceable sites. It is often the case that the best and easiest specimens to collect occur on scree slopes, fallen blocks, and waste tips; in-situ specimens are often difficult to remove and are easily destroyed and, therefore in some areas they would serve more people if left in their original position.

Good field workers record each fossil in detail, covering aspects of location and the relationship to sediments and to the associated fauna or flora. The collection of good specimens depends on the correct equipment; a geological hammer, chisels, brushes, pocket-knife, and hand lens are essential field tools. Storage boxes, wrapping paper, and plaster of Paris are also used for the care of specimens and particularly the transportation of delicate samples. After collection, it is best to move all specimens to a place where careful preparation may be undertaken, since cleaning or extraction of a fossil in the field will often result in unwanted damage. In the home or the laboratory, specimens can be prepared in a number of ways; the actual method of preparation depends on the fossil and the nature of the enclosing sediment. In the home, preparation is often restricted to simple mechanical techniques such as the use of strong needles or fine chisels. Even with these tools though, dedicated workers have freed exquisite specimens from the hardest rocks. In the modern laboratory, needles and chisels are supplemented by air abrasives, air-dents and the dentist's drill. For fossils embedded in shales and friable sandstones, needles and chisels will perform adequately, but for limestone and indurate sandstones, powered tools are usually necessary.

In many ways, the use of mechanical techniques has changed little since the early part of the nineteenth century. Acid or chemical methods are relatively new and have become increasingly important in the removal of fossils from harder rocks. However, these are essentially specialist techniques and should not be employed by inexperienced workers. Acids are used to dissolve the sediment, for example, dilute hydrochloric or acetic acids are used to extract siliceous, chitinous, or calcium phosphatic skeletons from limestones but prolonged washing in deionized and fresh water is necessary to remove the salts formed during chemical activity. Plastic-based glues are used during both mechanical and chemical preparation to protect specimens.

In establishing a worthwhile collection the curation of specimens is a major task and perhaps the most important. It involves both detective and clerical prowess, since the identification, labelling, and storage of specimens are all important for future reference. Fossils without locality data and, to a lesser extent, names are often useless and, therefore, individual specimens should be stored, numbered, and card-indexed with great care. Cards related to each specimen must display details of field locality and systematic position; the identification of the fossil being obtained by reference to monographs, treatises, or pocket-guides such as this. Accurate identification of individual fossils gives great satisfaction and helps the collector understand more about a particular family tree or evolutionary lineage.

Through the collection, preparation, and curation of various specimens, palaeontologists learn a great deal about the structure and character of individual fossils and their groups. This data together with evidence obtained in the field enables fossils to be associated with various environments; spines, ribs, thickness of shell, and shape of eyes, all being important clues in functional and environmental interpretations. The study of ancient associations and modes of life is one of the more exciting areas of palaeontology. However, in order to be a good palaeoecologist, it is first necessary to have a sound knowledge of the morphology and stratigraphical distribution of fossils.

As stated previously, the majority of fossils are found in sediments deposited in the sea or other aquatic environments. In part this is a reflection of the numbers of creatures that lived in the shallow seas throughout geological time. This abundance is also reflected in the chart on page 7 which attempts to show the distribution of marine organisms in contemporary environments. Through the detailed study of sediments and fossils, palaeontologists can construct similar diagrams for ancient environments.

Key to the identification of fossil organisms

Part 1

1 a	Solitary	pass to 2
b	Colonial	pass to 3
2 a	Non-chambered	pass to 4
b	Chambered	pass to 5
3 a	With pores	pass to 18
b	Without pores	pass to 19
4 a	Coiled	pass to gastropods (G2)
b	Non-coiled	pass to 6
5 a	Coiled	pass to 7
b	Non-coiled	pass to 8
6 a	Shell composed of single skeletal component	pass to 10
b	Shell composed of more than one skeletal component	pass to 13
7 a	Chamber partitions straight slightly curved	pass to 8
b	Chamber partitions folded	pass to ammonoids (G4)
8 a	Chamber partitions with small tube-like structure, the siphuncle	pass to 9
b	Small to microscopic organisms, siphuncle absent	pass to foraminiferids (A)
9 a	Chamber partitions (septa) straight or slightly curved	pass to nautiloids (G3)
b	Chamber partitions folded	pass to ammonoids (G4)
10 a	With radial symmetry	pass to 11
b	Without radial symmetry	pass to 12
11 a	With vertical radiating partitions	pass to solitary corals (D2—3)
b	Solid with central tube radiate pattern	pass to crinoids (H4)

12 a Unit large with large aperature, pores present, single wall	pass to solitary sponges (B)
b Unit large with large aperture, pores, double wall	pass to archaeocyathids (C)
c Unit large with large aperture	pass to gastropods (G2)
d Microscopic to small	pass to foraminiferids (A)
13 a Bilateral symmetry	pass to 14
b Radial symmetry	pass to 16
14 a Shell composed of two valves	pass to 15
b Segmented skeleton	pass to arthropods (I)
15 a Two valves, usually mirror image of each other and usually of equal size	pass to bivalves (G1)
b Valves usually of different sizes not mirror images, equilateral symmetry	pass to brachiopods (F)
16 a Radial symmetry follows five-fold plan	pass to 17
b Radial symmetry without five-fold level of organization	pass to solitary corals (D23)
17 a Skeleton with arms and with or without stem	pass to crinoids (H2) pass to blastoids (H3)
b Skeleton rounded or plate-like arms incorporated into test	pass to echinoids (H1)
c Flattened with five radiating arms	pass to starfish (H4)
18 a With single porus wall	pass to sponges (B)
19 a Laminate structure, box-like units	pass to stromatoporoids
b Tube or box-like units	pass to 20
20 a Large with vertical radial partitions	pass to corals (D1−2−3)
b No radiating vertical partitions, small to microscopic in size	pass to 21
21 a Rod-like branches	pass to graptolites (J)
b Moss-like with many small apertures	pass to bryozoans (E)

Part II

A Protozoa (Foraminiferida-Radiolaria)

Microscopic to small, unicellular organisms which secrete a calcareous or siliceous shell. The shell may be composed of a solitary chamber or a multiple of chambers.

B Porifera (Sponges)

Multicellular animals which secrete calcareous or siliceous spicules that are often fused together to form a rigid skeleton. Characterized by a large common opening, the **osculum**, and numerous pores. Colonial and solitary sponges are known from the geological record.

C Archaeocyathids

Extinct Cambrian organisms characterized by a cone in cone wall structure. Both walls have a porous nature.

D Coelenterata (Corals)

Close relatives of the sea-anemone which secrete calcareous skeletons with horizontal and vertical partitions (**tabulae** and **septa**). Tabulate (D1) corals exclusively colonial, while rugose and scleractine corals (D2 and D3) include both colonial and solitary forms.

The stromatoporoids (D4) are also members of this phylum but their laminate structure separates them from the corals noted above.

E Bryozoa

Mostly small to microscopic colonial organisms, often called the moss animals. Their structure is very variable, some resemble graptolites while others are massive and coral-like.

F Brachiopoda

Shell made-up of two valves of unequal size but with an equilateral symmetry. The shell may be composed of calcite or chitinophosphatic substances.

G Mollusca

Important group of invertebrates which includes several subgroups for example: bivalves (G1), with two valves usually of equal size; gastropods (G2), with single shell unit, which is either coiled or straight but always un-chambered; nautiloids (G3), which have either straight or coiled shells, the shells are chambered with the chambers separated by straight partitions; and ammonoids (G4), with straight or coiled shells, which are chambered with folded partitions.

H Echinodermata

The skeletons are made-up of interlocking calcareous plates and are character-ized by a five-fold symmetry. In the echinoids (H1) the test is usually sub-rounded to plate-like; the arms being incorporated into the overall structure. The skeleton of the crinoids (H2) and blastoids (H3) is divided into a cup, arms, and stem. Both the arms and the stem of crinoids are made-up of numerous ossicles which are extremely abundant at certain stratigraphic horizons. Other echinoderms known from the stratigraphic record include the starfish and brittle stars (H4).

I Arthropoda

Characterized by segmented skeletons with jointed limbs. Modern repre-sentatives include the crabs and lobsters, while the trilobites were very important during the Palaeozoic era. The trilobites have a bilateral symmetry and can be divided into head, thorax, and tail regions.

J Graptolithina

Colonial organisms with numerous individual cups arranged along rod-like branches. Number of branches may vary from one to several hundreds.

This key is intended to help the collector identify invertebrate fossils to group level. It is not designed to help in the identification of either plants or vertebrates. This and the naming of invertebrate specimens at **generic** and **specific** level will require further research in libraries and museums.

The majority of specimens discovered in field locations would fall within the measure stated in the text. Also, a few specimens are displayed in a non-classic position in order to emphasize their structure.

Protozoa

The most important group of proto-zoans, from a palaeontological view-point, are the Foraminiferida. Like their relative the *Amoeba*, the foraminiferids are single-celled animals, but unlike *Amoeba* they secrete skeletons. The latter may result from the cementing together of sedimentary particles (ag-glutination) or by the deposition of a calcareous shell or **test**. Chitinous or agglutinated forms were dominant in the Lower Palaeozoic but by the Carboniferous, calcareous forms were abundant. Most foraminiferids are microscopic in size although groups such as the fusulinids (Carboniferous — Permian) and nummulitids (Eocene — Oligocene) grew to significant pro-portions. These and other forms were complex in character, the test being made up of numerous **chambers**. Features such as the mode of coiling, internal structures, and the compo-sition of the test wall are important in the classification of the Foraminiferida.

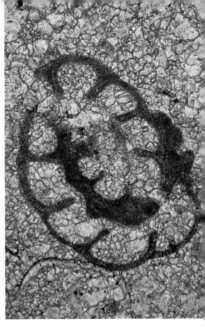

Endothyra

Europe, Americas, Africa, Japan
Lower Carboniferous — Permian
Diameter 0·5–1 mm

Endothyra is a member of the ex-tremely important suborder Fusulinina, which are used for the stratigraphic correlation of Upper Palaeozoic strata. It has an enrolled test in which the outer whorls slightly overhang the inner ones (involute). The coiling of the test varies slightly during growth, and nodes and fine ridges may occur over the surface of the outer whorls. Although layered in structure, recrystal-lization does give the test a rather granular texture. It is often difficult to see the aperture which is often mar-ginal and slit-like. Where the test exhibits erratic coiling the outer cham-bers are displaced from the midline. *Endothyra* and related genera reached their acme during Upper Carboniferous and Permian times; no members of the Fusulinina survived into the Jurassic period.

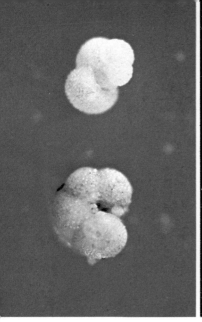

Globigerina

Worldwide
Palaeocene – Recent
Microscopic

Globigerina is a foraminiferid in which the chambers are spirally coiled. On one side of the test the chambers overlap each other while on the other, they tend to exhibit uncoiling. The chambers of *Globigerina* are spherical to oval in shape, and the wall has a radial structure pierced by numerous fine perforations. The external ornament of the genus varies from smooth to pitted or even spinose. A large aperture is characteristic of *Globigerina*, and it is found in approximately the middle of the test on the uncoiled surface. Species referred to the genus first occur in rocks 60 million years old, but fossils belonging to the superfamily Globigerinacaea are known from Middle Jurassic sediments. The globigerinids are planktonic organisms, various living species being diagnostic of either warm or cold environments.

Nummulites

Worldwide
Palaeocene – Oligocene
Width 3–20 mm

The tests of species in the genus *Nummulites* vary considerably in size and may be lens-like or discoidal in shape. They are also flattened and usually involute. Each test consists of a large number of whorls coiled in a spiral plane, with numerous chambers present in each whorl. The whorls are divided by well-developed septa and a sectioned test reveals that these are usually directed backwards, towards the protoconch (initial chamber area). The surface ornament varies from smooth to moderately ribbed, and the various patterns are used in the identification of species. As larger foraminiferids, the nummulitids are very important in Eocene stratigraphy, and species such as *N. planulatus*, *N. laevigatus*, and *N. variolarius* are important zone fossils.

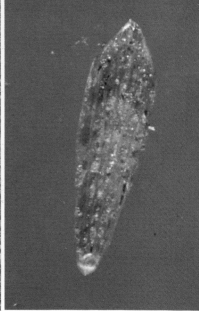

Alveolina (Borelis)

Europe, Asia, Africa
Upper Eocene — Recent
Width 1—3 mm

The family Alveolinidae, named after the genus *Alveolina*, was important during the Cainozoic era. Genera referred to the group are included in the general term 'larger Foraminiferida', with the genus *Fasciolites* reaching 100 mm in length. The tests of the alveolinids are coiled around an elongate axis and have a fusiform to spherical shape. A large number of chambers is typical, with individual chambers subdivided into smaller tubular ones. The wall of the test is calcareous with the surface having a white shiny appearance similar to that of porcelain (**porcelaneous**). In recent years the name *Alveolina* has been termed a junior synonym of the genus *Borelis*; this does not, however, affect the name of the family or the 'sack term' alveolinid.

Frondicularia

Worldwide
Permian — Recent
Length 0·5—1 mm

Frondicularia is a member of a very important suborder of the foraminiferids called the Rotaliina. It has a calcareous test with many chambers which have an arrangement similar to that of a palm leaf; the test is elongate and flat, and the chambers are low and broad. In *Frondicularia*, the aperture is found in the terminal position, but in some species it is raised beyond the test by the presence of a short neck. The aperture also has a radiate structure in which the opening is associated with a number of diverging slits. *F. cordai* is a well-known species from the Lower Chalk of the Upper Cretaceous. Rotalinid foraminiferids are very important in the correlation of post-Palaeozoic sediments.

Porifera — Sponges

The sponges represent the simplest level of multicellular animals and use both calcite and silica in construction of the skeleton. They range from the Precambrian period to the present day, and fossil evidence of the sponges may vary from the discovery of individual **spicules** to that of large solitary vase-like structures. Fossil sponges, like their contemporary cousins, were either solitary or colonial and characterized by many **pores**. The spicules noted above are the building blocks of the sponge. They vary considerably in size and shape with various types being characteristic of a given group, and when fused together form a rigid skeleton. The sponges have no mouth or anus but a common opening, the **osculum**, is present on the upper surface. Sponges with siliceous skeletons probably lived in deeper colder waters than those with calcareous ones.

Siphonia

Europe
Middle Cretaceous — Tertiary
Length 15–20 cm

Siphonia is a member of the siliceous demosponges, a class of sponges characterized by a complex structure. It is included in the order Lithistida, individuals of which are noted for having large lumpy spicules called **desmas** which are interlocked or cemented to give a rigid framework. *Siphonia* is a stalked sponge of fairly large proportions and the body is rather tulip-like, with a small to moderate-sized osculum on the upper surface. Its exterior is smooth with numerous small pores. In section, the body has a dense structure pocked with regularly arranged chambers which connect with the main central chamber and the osculum. The stem is long within large rooting structures. *S. tulipa* is found in Upper Cretaceous beds.

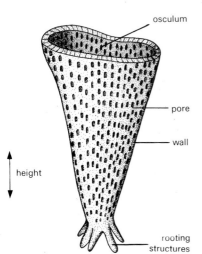

osculum

pore

wall

height

rooting structures

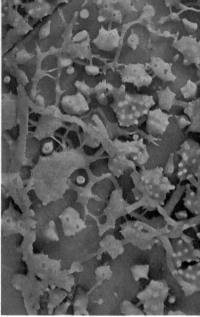

Doryderma

Europe
Carboniferous — Upper Cretaceous
Height of branched individuals
  15–30 cm

Doryderma is a rather massive compact and complex siliceous sponge belonging to the class Demospongea. The spicules (desmas) have a large rather lumpy character and are usually locked or cemented together to form a rigid framework. *Doryderma* has a branched plant-like appearance with numerous cylindrical branches arising from a main 'stem'. The branches are rather short and at least 1 cm in diameter, and each one has its own osculum or large opening through which water and waste materials were expelled. Although it has a long stratigraphic range, *Doryderma* was particularly abundant during the Upper Cretaceous period. Modern representatives of the group to which *Doryderma* is referred, live mainly below the zone of light penetration in most marine systems.

Entobia (Cliona)

Worldwide
Devonian — Recent
Diameter of burrows 1–6 mm

Like *Siphonia*, *Entobia* is a siliceous demosponge. It has, however, a very different structure as it belongs to a family of burrowing sponges. In life, the soft parts of *Entobia* have a radiate structure, which is bounded by a thick leathery external cover. The skeleton is formed of both small and large spicules, **microscleres** and **megascleres**, respectively. Both types of spicules have a star-like structure, but the rays of the megascleres are swollen at the tips. As a burrowing sponge, *Entobia* excavates shallow meandering galleries. These burrows are often made on the surface of calcareous shells although some of the best examples are found preserved in Cretaceous flints. The species *E. cretacea* is particularly well known from the chalk deposits of Europe.

Ventriculites

Europe
Middle — Upper Cretaceous
Diameter 5—8 cm

Ventriculites is a member of the 'glass sponges' or Hyalospongea, which are characterized by siliceous four-, five-, or six-rayed spicules. Its skeleton is rigid and the shape, although generally vase-like, varies from nearly cylindrical to saucer-like. The walls are rather thin and conspicuous canals can be noted running parallel to the long axis of the sponge. A large single osculum occupies the upper surface of the sponge, while the base is small and characterized by the presence of radiating rooting structures. Various species of *Ventriculites* are common in the Middle and Upper Cretaceous beds of Europe, with *V. striatus* (Germany) and *V. infundibuliformis* (England) being among the best known.

Corynella

Europe, possibly East Indies
Triassic — Cretaceous
Diameter of individual unit 4—16 mm

The genus *Corynella* is a member of the calcareous sponges of the order Pharetronida, and belongs to the same family as *Rhaphidonema*. Sponges included in this order are characterized by three-rayed spicules of the tuning-fork type. The spicules are interlocked or cemented together and the skeleton has a cylindrical or top-shaped form. Some individuals can be described as knobby and they may possess one or more oscula. *Corynella's* structure is complex and canals may or may not be evident. The species *C. quenstedi* is well known from the Upper Jurassic of Germany, while *C. foraminosa* is very common in the Lower Cretaceous of England.

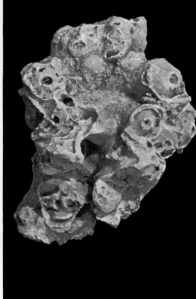

Rhaphidonema

Europe
Triassic — Cretaceous
Diameter of individual units 4—6 cm

Like *Corynella*, *Rhaphidonema* is a calcareous sponge of the order Pharetronida. The family to which they belong, the Lelapiidae, is characterized by either erect cylinder or inverted cone shapes; *Corynella* is more like the former while *Rhaphidonema* is like the latter. Vase-shaped or funnel-like would also describe this genus, the exterior of which is rough and somewhat lumpy or mammelate. Large pores can be distinguished on the outer surface while the inner surface is smoother and the pores are smaller. A single very large osculum is one of the most notable characters of this well-known form. *R. farringdonense* is named after the town of Farringdon, England, one of the most fossiliferous sponge localities in the world.

Tremacystia

England, France, Germany
Jurassic — Cretaceous
Length of individual unit 1—2 cm

This is a calcareous colonial sponge in which the colony consists of an irregular base and a number of vertical tube-like structures. The tubes are subdivided by partitions into a series of subglobular chambers, and pierced by a central (axial) canal. In some specimens the canal does not extend to the base of the colony. The walls of the skeleton have a robust structure and are built of slender three-rayed spicules. *Tremacystia* and related genera belong to the order Thalamida which are the most structurally elaborate of all the calcareous sponges. The well-known Cretaceous genus *Barroisia* also belongs to the same family and is colonial; others, including *Girtyocoelia* from the Carboniferous, are solitary forms.

Coelenterata

The corals are members of the phylum Coelenterata and are related to such animals as the sea-anemone and *Hydra*. Corals secrete skeletons of calcite which are frequently found as fossils. The corals arose during the early Palaeozoic, with the Tabulata sharing many niches with the Rugosa. Both of these groups became extinct at the end of the Palaeozoic; the Seleractinia being the dominant group of post-Palaeozoic corals.

The tabulates were **colonial** animals, with the individual skeletons (**corallites**) grouped together to form a **corallum**. Among the Rugosa and Scleractinia both **solitary** and colonial forms were common. The features used in the identification of corals occur within the outer wall and include: horizontal plates that may extend across the full internal width – **tabulae** vertical radially disposed structures – **septa**; small, flat or curved plates – **dissepiments**; and a rod-like, solid or spongy longitudinal structure – the **columella**

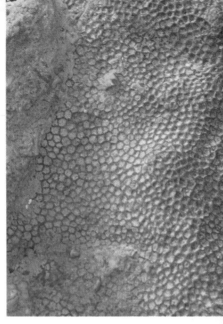

Tabulata

Favosites

Worldwide
Upper Ordovician – Middle Devonian
Width of individual corallite 1–3 mm

This is a massive tabulate coral in which the slender corallites are packed closely together. Individually, the corallites are prismatic in section and separated by thin walls. Pores in the midline of the walls link the corallites together. Small septa are present within each corallite as ridges or very short spines. As in other tabulate corals the major structures within the corallites are the tabulae, and in *Favosites* these are either flat or slightly convex forming a complete partition between the corallite walls. *Favosites* was one of the more common tabulates during the Silurian and Devonian periods, and in certain deposits formed a solid base for reef development together with other tabulate corals.

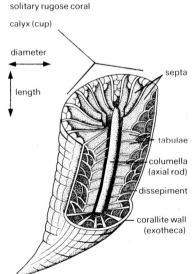

solitary rugose coral

calyx (cup)

diameter

length

septa

tabulae

columella (axial rod)

dissepiment

corallite wall (exotheca)

Syringopora

Worldwide
Silurian — Carboniferous
Individual corallite 1–3 mm

This coral forms large colonies composed of long cylindrical corallites which are irregularly branched. The erect corallites are connected by hollow transverse processes. Septa occur in certain species with twelve being the typical number. Unlike the septa of the rugose corals, those of *Syringopora* are small and spiny in character. The tabulae are numerous and closely packed with a deep depression in the central or axial area. A careful examination of the characters noted above should avoid confusion between *Syringopora* and some species of *Lithostrotion*. Both corals are known from Carboniferous deposits although *Syringopora* first appeared in the Silurian. *Syringopora* also lacks the dissepiments and axial boss, which are diagnostic of *Lithostrotion*.

Heliolites

Worldwide
Silurian — Middle Devonian
Individual corallite 0·5–1 mm

Heliolites is among the best known of tabulate corals. Like *Favosites* and *Syringopora* it is colonial but the organization of the skeleton gives it a degree of individuality. The colony consists of large corallites bounded by a number of small tube-like structures. Each tube has its own thin walls and horizontal partitions and more than twelve bound each larger unit. The larger units are like the corallites of *Favosites* with small spinose septa present. In longitudinal section, the corallites are seen to have complete horizontal tabulae. *Heliolites* was a prominent member of shallow-water communities for over 50 million years. Other tabulate corals such as *Favosites* and *Syringopora* are often found in the same sediments as this genus.

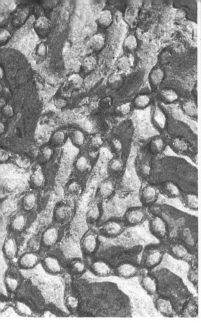

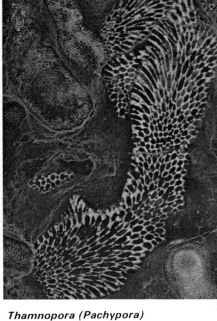

Halysites

Almost worldwide
Ordovician — Silurian
Individual corallite 1–1·5 mm

Frequently called the 'chain coral', *Halysites* consists of a number of elongate corallites linked along the entire length of the adjoining edges and united to give a chain-like surface pattern. Unlike *Favosites* it has no mural pores and septa are not a noticeable feature. The tabulae of *Halysites* are usually horizontal although they may be slightly arched in some specimens. In cross-section, the individual corallites are circular in outline, a smaller corallite often occurring between two larger ones. The majority of *Halysites* specimens are found in limestone deposits. Only three genera form the family Halysitidae, and the other two genera *Labyrinthes* and *Arcturia* are found only in North America.

Thamnopora (Pachypora)

Worldwide
Silurian — Permian
Individual corallite 1–1·5 mm

Although the genus *Thamnopora* is known to have occurred throughout the world during this period, one species *T. cervicornis*, is restricted to Europe during the Middle Devonian. *Thamnopora* formed massive colonies in which the walls of the corallites became thicker as the corallum developed. The corallites are short and closely packed, branching frequently to give a characteristic form. Septa are poorly developed in *Thamnopora* and are rather spinose in appearance. Numerous pores link individual corallites and large numbers of thin tabulae also occur. The vast majority of specimens are found in limestones that were deposited on the continental shelf. The massive colonies may be tuberose or branching in character.

Tryplasma

Europe, Asia, North America,
  Australia
Silurian — Lower Devonian
Length of corallite 2–3 cm

A small rugose coral, *Tryplasma*, is a
solitary form in which the septa are
short but numerous. The dissepiments
occur in numbers around the outer
edge of the cup, occupying a distinct
band approximately two-thirds the
width of the septal length. This band is
also noticeable in the vertical section
as are the tabulae which are horizontal
with an occasional notch in the midline. In many examples of *Tryplasma*
distinct rims are present along the
length of the corallite. These represent
a change in the growth pattern of the
individual which is called **rejuvenation**.
Many corals related to *Tryplasma* lack
dissepiments.

Petraia

Europe
Upper Silurian
Diameter of corallite 10–15 mm

Petraia is a small solitary rugose coral
noted for having long thin septa that
meet at the centre of the corallite.
Small minor septa clearly alternate with
the long major septa. A deep cup-like
depression represents the area previously occupied by the anemone-like
soft parts. Only a few tabulae are
present within this form. It is possible
that *Petraia* and its relatives lived in
rather deeper waters than their larger
colonial cousins of later times. Numerous individuals of *Petraia*, often de-
calcified, can be found in deposits from
Western Europe. In such specimens, the
septa protrude and it is often necessary
to take a cast in order to study the true
structure of the cup.

Acervularia

Europe
Silurian
Diameter of corallite 6–15 mm

This rugose coral forms massive colonies in which the individual units (corallites) are closely united and polygonal in shape. Both septa and dissepiments are easily recognizable with the ends of the minor septa forming a distinct wall outside the central area of the corallite. The dissepiments are organized into three distinct zones, and the major septa are long, a circular depression in the centre of the fossil marking their inner boundary. Many colonies of *Acervularia* exhibit the budding of four young corallites in the axis of a parent structure. *Acervularia* thrived in warm shallow-water environments that existed during the Silurian period. The species *A. ananas* from the Wenlock Series is named after the pineapple to which it bears some modest resemblance.

Calceola

Worldwide
Lower – Middle Devonian
Average length 3–4 cm
Average width 2–4 cm

Like *Goniophyllum*, *Calceola* is a small solitary rugose coral characterized by the presence of an operculum or lid. The individual corallite is somewhat slipper-shaped, curving slightly upwards at the narrower end. Unlike *Goniophyllum*, *Calceola* has a single semicircular plate acting as the operculum; its shape reflects the semicircular section of the corallite. The lower surface is flat with a transverse ornament of growth ridges. In life, it is thought that this coral lived with the broader end directed into the prevailing current; the development of the operculum and the broad flat base being possible adaptations to this mode of life. The calyx of *Calceola* is relatively shallow, the major septa of the upper and lateral surfaces being larger than those of the lower one.

Goniophyllum
Europe
Silurian
Width 10–15 mm

An unusual rugose coral in which the corallite has a square cross-section. Within the outer wall there is a wide area occupied by thickened dissepiments. The septa are also thick and appear as long as the width of the dissepiment area. A large number of tabulae are also present within each corallite. Like its relative *Calceola*, *Goniophyllum* has a lid-like cover over the cup of the corallite. In *Goniophyllum*, however, the lid is composed of four small triangular plates. The name *G. pyramidale* aptly describes the species found only in the Lower and Middle Silurian of Europe. The specific name is drawn from the term **pyramidal** which is used to describe the shape of the corallite.

Hexagonaria
Worldwide
Devonian
Width across corallite 4–10 mm

The corallum of *Hexagonaria* is massive and the walls of the individual corallites are closely united. Within the strong outer walls the septa are long, sometimes having lateral outgrowths (carinae). The septa may meet and entwine in the axial region. In many field discoveries a weathered pit is a notable feature of each corallite. A number of small globose dissepiments occur on the outside of the pit area. Externally, the corallites are ornamented by strong horizontal ridges and the vertical lines of the septa. The individual corallites are usually five-sided, but four- and six-sided individuals may occur within the compacted corallum. A number of finds in Asia suggest that *Hexagonaria* also persisted into the Carboniferous period.

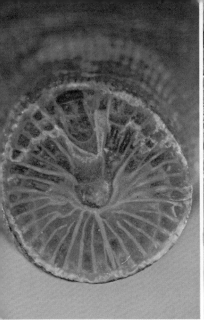

Zaphrentites (Zaphrentis)

Europe, Asia
Lower Carboniferous
Length of corallite 2·5–4 cm

A small- to medium-sized solitary coral which has a horn-shaped coral-lite. The major septa are elongate and meet just outside the axial area. A large interseptal space is common to the genus; this space occurs on the inside (curved) surface of the corallite. Minor septa are relatively unimportant since they are very short or even absent in some species. Individual specimens of *Zaphrentites* are often discovered in limestones that were deposited in shallow-water environments. Sections through a corallite, from its tip to the widest point, may reveal the manner in which the septa were emplaced during growth. In certain species the septa are extremely short, and in some regions of the world the various species have been used for zonation.

Lithostrotion

Worldwide
Lower–Middle Carboniferous
Diameter of individual corallite
3–15 mm

The generic name *Lithostrotion* is given to a number of species of Carbon-iferous coral which grew in shallow-water environments. Each of the species was colonial; the individual corallites varying from round to hexagonal in section. Several characters such as a small rod-like central structure and short thick septa help in the classifi-cation and association of the various species. In comparison with other corals, the individual units of *Lithos-trotion* are small to medium in size, the largest corallites having a diameter of 8–10 mm. *Lithostrotion* also has fewer dissepiments than many contemporary corals.

Caninia

Europe, North America, Asia,
　Australia
Carboniferous — Permian
Diameter of individual corallite
　3–8 cm

Caninia is a medium- to large-sized
solitary coral found relatively abundant
in Carboniferous rocks. It is either
cylindrical or like an elongate cone in
shape, with distinct growth lines as
external ornament. The septa vary with
the age of the specimen, becoming
shorter and less dilated in the adult
stages. Dissepiments are less common
than in other forms, but a distinct, thin
band of plates may occur around the
outer edge. The tabulae of *Caninia* are
flat, and are most noticeable in weathered specimens. This weathering may
give the outer edge a very rough texture. The very large form *C. gigantea* is
also known under the name of *Siphon-
ophyllia gigantea*.

Dibunophyllum

Europe, North Africa, North America
Lower–Middle Carboniferous
Diameter of individual corallite
　2–3 cm

A medium- to large-sized solitary
coral, *Dibunophyllum*, is a useful
stratigraphic fossil and is easily recognizable through the form of its complex
axial area. This area is one-third as
wide as the corallite and is rather web-
like in appearance. Outside this central
zone one notices that there are a large
number of septa the ends of which fuse
into the central web. Abundant dissepiments are also a feature of *Dibunophyllum*. These are usually small and
form a wide band around the corallite.
The minor septa of this coral are of
reduced significance. Longitudinal
lines, corresponding to the septa and
circular growth lines, may ornament
the outer surface of the corallite.

Scleractinia

Isastrea

Europe, Africa, North America
Middle Jurassic — Cretaceous
Diameter of individual corallite
    3–5 mm

Thecosmilia

Worldwide
Triassic — Cretaceous
Length of individual 'branch' 5–12 cm

This is a massive colonial coral where the individual corallites are closely packed together with the outer wall formed either by the ends of the septa or by closely packed dissepiments. In some species, however, the outer wall is missing and the septa from adjacent corallites may run into each other. Most corallites have five or six sides. Inside the corallite walls there are numerous septa of differing lengths, the upper edges of which have a beaded appearance. *Isastrea* has no central columella. Individual colonies are often rounded and about the size of a small plate. *Isastrea* is often found in association with *Thamnasteria* and various brachiopods, including rhynchonellids. It is likely that they existed in shallow-water environments.

The colonies of *Thecosmilia* are made up of large broad corallites with circular cross-sections which individually resemble *Montlivaltia*. They are also cylindrical and arranged in a subparallel formation, with limited contact with each other. In individual corallites the septa are numerous and well defined, whereas the columnella is either very weak or absent. Numerous dissepiments are also present and clearly visible between septa. The outer wall is marked by fine growth lines but appears rather patchy in its development. Compared with other corals illustrated in this guide the individual corallites of *Thecosmilia* attain massive proportions. Several species of *Thecosmilia* were common in Europe during the Upper Jurassic.

Montlivaltia

Worldwide
Triassic — Cretaceous
Diameter 2·5—5 cm

Montlivaltia is a solitary scleractinian in which the corallites are large and circular in cross-section and may be horn-shaped, conical, or cylindrical lacking any indication of rooting or fixing structures. Externally, the skeleton is often characterized by the vertical ridges of the septa, the outer wall having been eroded away. The septa are long and numerous with a granular texture and small dentitions on their upper surface give them a serrated appearance. Numerous dissepiments are present and a weakly-developed columella occurs in the axial area. As with other scleractinians the septa may overlap the outer wall, but this feature is never witnessed in either the rugose or the tabulate corals.

Trochocyathus

Worldwide
Upper Jurassic — Recent
Diameter 3—5 mm

Like *Parasmilia*, this is a small scleractinian coral which has representation in the seas of the present day. *Trochocyathus* varies in shape from that of a small turban-like structure to one which is slender and horn-shaped. Both major and minor septa are visible, with the major units reaching as far as the columella. A distinct outer wall, the **epitheca** surrounds the septa in this genus. The columella is generally small with a spongy texture. *Trochocyathus* lives today in a number of environments; various species being found between 35—1 500 m in depth. It is possible that the earliest representatives in the Middle Jurassic were more restricted in their depth ranges. Some specimens of *Trochocyathus* lived in a fixed position, while others rested free on the sediment of the sea-floor.

Parasmilia

Worldwide
Cretaceous — Recent
Length of corallite 1·5–3 cm

Parasmilia is a rather small solitary coral, contemporary representatives of which live at a depth of approximately 325 m. In cross-section the corallite is circular, while in longitudinal section it has a horn-shaped profile. The septa are numerous and characterized by a granular surface texture. The centre of the corallite is occupied by a large spongy axial structure. Dissepiments are developed in *Parasmilia* but are only found deep within the corallite. Externally, the skeleton is marked by deep vertical ridges and at the base a flattened attachment area is clearly visible. Individual specimens are sedentary, being fixed either to the substrate or to other organisms.

Sphenotrochus

Worldwide
Eocene — Recent
Length of corallite 4–8 mm

This small solitary coral has existed for the last 60 million years. It is somewhat wedge-shaped with the outer surface marked either by strong vertical ridges or granulations. Two types of septa are visible, the minor septa are short, while the major septa terminate close to the broad columella. Recent species from the Indian Ocean live at depths ranging from 80–140 m. *Sphenotrochus* is not a reef-dwelling coral. The species *S. intermedius* is well known from the Pliocene deposits of Europe. *Sphenotrochus* is closely related to the equally small coral *Turbinolia*, which is abundant in various Tertiary deposits of Europe. Corals that live outside the reef-building environment are termed **ahermatypic**.

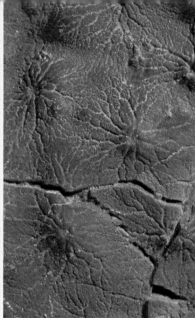

Goniopora
Europe, Pacific Region
Cretaceous — Recent
Diameter of corallite 2—4 mm

Goniopora is a massive colonial coral. The corallites may be straight or branching, they are closely packed within the corallum, and their outer walls have a thick granular appearance. The septa also have a granular texture with three cycles of septa known in this genus. In some instances, the innermost areas of the septa become separated to form ridges or **pali**. To some extent these resemble the columella of other corals. *Goniopora* first appeared in the Middle Cretaceous and is found today in Pacific waters. It is a reef-dwelling coral common in shallow-shelf seas. Several species occur in the Tertiary rocks of Europe, with *G. websteri* representing the genus in Lutetian times.

Stromatoporoid
Worldwide
Carboniferous — Cretaceous
Width across canal system 1—6 mm

The stromatoporoids are, as coelenterates, related to the various coral genera described in this text. They are colonial organisms with a rather dense-layered skeleton of calcite. The size of the colony is variable and their structure is a useful indicator of conditions that prevailed during the lifetime of the organisms. Successive layers of the colony, especially stromatoporoid, are characterized by the presence of pronounced mounds (monticules) and a series of root-like canals (astrorhizae). Together, these structures have a star-like pattern. The absence of septa and tabulae separates the stromatoporoids from the corals; most palaeontologists place the group with the hydrozoan coelenterates. As fossils, the stromatoporoids are important in reef building during the Silurian and Devonian periods.

Bryozoa or Polyzoa

Frequently referred to as the 'moss animals', the Bryozoa are colonial creatures, in which individuals are extremely small in size. Colonies may be delicate lace-like structures or massive and coral-like in appearance. The bryozoans have existed since the Late Cambrian and are found mainly in shales and limestones. A colony of bryozoans is termed the **zoarium**, with each of the individual tubes being called a **zooecium**. Each tube has an **aperture**, which may or may not be covered with a lid or **operculum**. Internal structures such as cross-partitions or **diaphragms** are used in classification, as are some external features and a variety of modified zooecia.

The bryozoans are subdivided into five groups, namely the Cryptostomata (Ordovician — Permian), Trepostomata (Ordovician — Permian), Ctenostomata (Ordovician — Recent), Cyclostomata (Ordovician — Recent) and Cheilostomata (Jurassic — Recent) and most are important in reef building.

Fenestella

Europe
Ordovician — Permian
Width of individual branch
0·3—0·5 mm

Fenestella is a member of the so-called 'lace bryozoans', the colonies of which bear a close resemblance to the material of that name. The colony consists of numerous almost parallel branches which are slender and connected at intervals by thin crossbars called **dissepiments**. Numerous zooecia are situated on one side of the lace-like network; these have rounded openings and only occur on the vertical branches. In most species the zoarium is fan-shaped or funnel-like. *Fenestella* and its relatives are very common in the Upper Palaeozoic, especially in the muddy lime-rich sediments of the Carboniferous.

Bryozoa colony (zoarium)

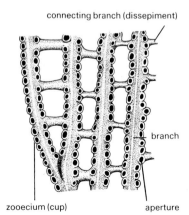

connecting branch (dissepiment)

branch

zooecium (cup)

aperture

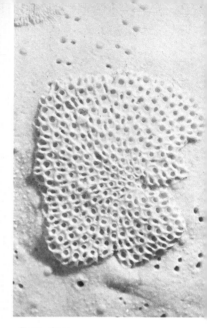

Archimedes

Europe, North America, Asia
Carboniferous – Permian
Coil width 0·5–2 cm

Archimedes belongs to the same family
of bryozoans as *Fenestella*. In both
forms the colonies consist of rigid
branches which are joined laterally by
regularly placed dissepiments (crossbars). *Fenestella* has a rather simple
frond structure but *Archimedes* is
unique in that fronds are twisted
around a spiral axis. This coiling is
achieved by the localized deposition of
skeletal tissue which provides the delicate lace-like frond with axial support.
The branches of *Archimedes* are characterized by the presence of two rows
of apertures on the upper surface. The
twisting of the fronds around the spiral
axis makes *Archimedes* one of the most
recognizable of all bryozoans. Most of
the species referred to this genus occur
in rocks of Carboniferous age.

Berenicea

Europe, Africa, North America
Ordovician – Recent
Diameter 1–2 cm

Berenicea is characterized by a circular
to subcircular colony in which the
individual zooecia appear to radiate
from a central point. The colony has
the form of a low encrusting disc and
is often found attached to pebbles or
the shells of other organisms. Individually, the zooecia have rather thick
walls and a rounded aperture. They are
also tubular and closely packed, which
tends to disguise the fact that they
radiate along irregular lines. *Berenicea*
has a long geological range and
reaches a peak, in terms of numbers,
during the Jurassic and Cretaceous
periods. The identification of species
is a difficult task, but common forms,
such as *B. archiaci* from the Jurassic,
are found in a number of more specialist
texts.

Brachiopoda

The brachiopods possess a two-valved chitinophosphatic or calcareous shell. Both valves have an equilateral symmetry but the pedicle valve is larger than the brachial one. The brachiopods are divided into two major groups based on the composition and structure of the shell: the inarticulata have a chitinophosphatic shell and lack teeth or any internal support structures, while the Articulata possess a calcareous shell and have a well-developed **hinge line**. **Teeth** and **sockets** are present and internal support structures are developed to a varying degree in different stocks. In the description of an articulate shell, the anterior or front is the area where the valves open. Posteriorly, one may find two pronounced **beaks** and between the beaks and the hinge line distinct flat platforms called **interareas**. An opening for the **pedicle** characterizes the pedicle valve, and concentric growth lines and radiating ridges may ornament both shells.

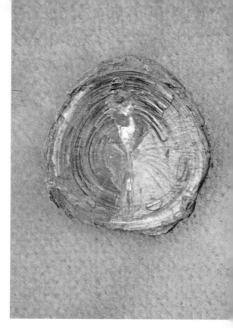

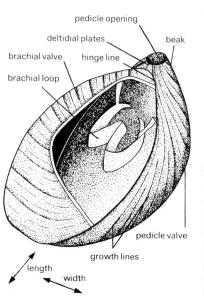

pedicle opening
deltidial plates
beak
brachial valve
hinge line
brachial loop
pedicle valve
growth lines
length
width

Orbiculoidea

Worldwide
Ordovician — Permian
Large specimens up to 12 mm

Like *Lingulella*, *Orbiculoidea* is an inarticulate brachiopod. It belongs, however, to a different order many genera of which are characterized by concentric growth, with the increase in valve size taking place around the complete margin of the valves. This growth pattern is reflected in the concentric ornament typically found in *Orbiculoidea*, which also has a rounded chitinophosphatic shell. The brachial valve of this genus is conical to subconical with the apex occurring in an almost central position. Concentric growth lines are also present on the flattened to concave pedicle valve, which is recognized by the presence of a short closed pedicle track. In some species, a low ridge may occur in the middle of the brachial valve which extends from the apex towards the anterior edge of the valve.

Lingula

Worldwide
Ordovician — Recent
Length 1–4 cm

Lingula, an inarticulate brachiopod, has a geological record rivalled by few animals. As an inarticulate it has a chitinophosphatic shell made up of two equal valves which are elongate and marked with fine growth lines. The hinge area is short, and the main mechanism for opening the valves is a series of strong muscles, the scars of which can be observed in well-preserved specimens. Most fossils of *Lingula* are discovered in shale deposits, the shells having a lustrous black appearance. In a few cases, fossil lingulids have been found preserved in the burrows they occupied in life.

Heterorthis

Europe, North America
Middle — Upper Ordovician
Width 1·5–3 cm

Heterorthis is a member of the orthid brachiopods which to many people are the least specialized of the articulates. It has a roughly subcircular shape with the maximum width occurring in front of the hinge line. The shell is noted for having a convex pedicle valve, while the brachial valve is either concave or flat. A well-developed triangular plate is present covering the pedicle opening on the brachial valve. Internally, it is often possible to identify the muscle scars on the surface of the pedicle valve. The external surface of *Heterorthis* is ornamented by strong radiating ribs and fine concentric growth lines. *H. alternata* is a well-known species from Middle Ordovician sediments.

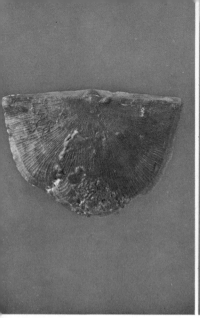

Strophomena

Worldwide
Middle — Upper Ordovician
Width 3–4 cm

Like other members of the order to which it gives its name (Strophomenida), *Strophomena* has a convex brachial valve and a concave pedicle valve. Interareas are also present on both valves, with that of the pedicle valve being larger than that of the brachial one. The hinge line is very long and occupies the widest part of the shell. Externally, the valves are ornamented by fine radiating ridges which are cut by concentric growth lines. No large internal support structures characterize the brachial valve of *Strophomena*. The microstructure of the shell is also important in the classification of strophomenids. Under a microscope the shell is seen to be pockmarked, due to the presence of numerous closely packed pseudopunctae.

Pentamerus

Europe, North America, Asia
Silurian
Length 2·5–6 cm

Unlike the related genus *Conchidium*, *Pentamerus* is confined to rocks of Silurian age. It is, however, a typical pentamerid being rather large and biconvex. *Pentamerus* has a smooth surface with an ornament of fine concentric growth lines. The beak of the pedicle valve is stronger and much larger in its development than that of the brachial valve. Both valves are comparatively long, and no fold is present along the anterior opening. Internally, the midline muscle support structures are well developed, while the supports for the feeding organ are quite small. The dental plates of *Pentamerus* fuse to form a large rather spoon-shaped structure, the **spondylium**. In Europe, this genus is well known from the Lower Silurian of England and Sweden.

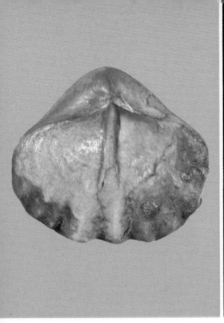

Gypidula

Northern Hemisphere
Lower Silurian — Upper Devonian
Width 2–3 cm

Together with *Pentamerus* and *Conchidium*, the presence of *Gypidula* illustrates the relative importance of the pentamerids during the periods in question. *Gypidula* belongs to a separate group from the other two; an anterior fold in the pedicle valve being a major factor in this division. The shell is elongate and subcircular in outline, with the pedicle valve rather inflated. Posteriorly, the pedicle beak is large and is seen to curve over the brachial valve. Internally, the support structures for the feeding organ can and have been described as 'lyre-shaped' in cross-section. The valve surfaces are ornamented by radiating ridges which are cut in the anterior region by distinct growth lines.

Leptaena

Worldwide
Middle Ordovician — Devonian
Width 2–4 cm

Leptaena is a strophomenid in which the shell undergoes an abrupt change of growth direction in the anterior region. In side view, this change is seen as angular bend in the two valves. The pedicle valve is convex while the brachial is concave. Posteriorly, the interareas are long and narrow with the hinge line equalling the maximum width of the shell. The surface ornament of the shell is characterized by pronounced concentric ridges (rugae) and a fine radiating ribbing. *L. rugosa* is a well-known species from the Upper Ordovician of Sweden and *L. rhomboidalis* is another from the Upper Silurian of England.

Sphaerirhynchia

Europe, possibly North America
Silurian
Width 8–15 mm

A small- to medium-sized rhynchonellid known essentially from the
Wenlockian of Northwest Europe.
Sphaerirhynchia is noted for its globose
somewhat cubic appearance, the front
and sides being flattened. Both valves
are strongly ribbed, with longitudinal
grooves present in the flattened areas
of the shell. The anterior opening, the
commissure, has the form of a broad
box-like fold. Posteriorly, the beak of
the pedicle valve, although small, is
quite prominent and turned slightly
inwards towards the brachial valve. In
some species, marginal spines may form
part of the shell ornament. Internally, a
pronounced septum forms part of the
brachial skeleton. The cardinal process,
characteristic of many rhynchonellids,
is missing in *Sphaerirhynchia*.

Atrypa

Worldwide
Lower Silurian – Upper Devonian
Width 1–2·5 cm

A small- to medium-sized spiriferid in
which the brachial valve is strongly
convex while the pedicle valve is
sometimes flattened or slightly concave. Both valves have an ornament of
longitudinal ridges which are crossed
by strong growth lines. The maximum
width of the shell is often at the hinge
line; the beak is small and directed
inwards. In large adult specimens the
shell may be more globose than in
juveniles, with a fringe developed
around the opening between the
valves. These changes may indicate a
different lifestyle, the older individuals
resting on their ventral valves; the
increased surface area prevented them
from sinking into the soft muds on
which they lived.

Conchidium

Worldwide
Upper Ordovician – Lower Devonian
Length 3–5 cm

A large pentamerid brachiopod whose valves, like those of other pentamerids, are extremely convex, with an ornament of strong ribs. The pedicle valve has a greater curvature than the brachial one and has a very strong beak, which overlaps the beak of the brachial valve. The interareas of both valves are rather small. Midline structures, such as a long spondylium, which developed on the inside of the shell make the collection of complete specimens of *Conchidium* difficult; a median split develops on extraction. The majority of specimens are collected from limestones deposited in shallow-water conditions. *C. knighti* from the Silurian beds is one of the best known of all the brachiopod species.

Chonetes

Worldwide
Devonian – Lower Carboniferous
Width 1–2·5 cm

Chonetes belongs to the same group of brachiopods as *Strophomena* and *Productus*. Unlike either of these forms, however, *Chonetes* has a concave pedicle valve. The hinge line corresponds to the greatest width of the shell in most species; the majority of forms being characterized by the presence of a number of short obliquely directed spines on the back edge of the pedicle valve. The brachial valve is convex, and has an interarea that is smaller than that of the pedicle valve. The external surface of the shell is ornamented with fine radiating ridges. Although *Chonetes* is recorded from rocks of Devonian and Lower Carboniferous age, the family to which it belongs is known to have existed from the Lower Silurian until the end of the Permian.

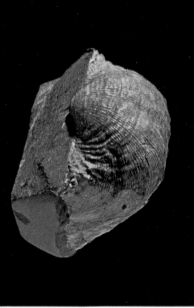

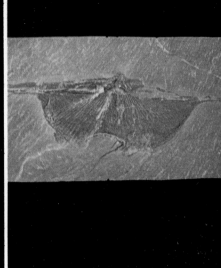

Productus

Europe, Asia
Lower – Upper Carboniferous
Width 2–25 cm

Productus is a medium- to large-sized brachiopod characterized by a sharp bend in the pedicle valve which is extremely convex while the brachial valve is flat. Both valves are heavily ribbed, with the ribbing being stronger than the concentric growth lines. Posteriorly, the pedicle valve is seen to overlap the hinge line and two rows of spines ornament the hinge area. Other spines or spine bases are also found scattered over the broader surface of the pedicle valve. In Europe, the majority of productids are found in limestones of the Lower Carboniferous series. In some forms the pedicle spines are very long and abundant, their function being to stabilize the shell on the seabed in fast moving currents.

Cyrtospirifer

Worldwide
Upper Devonian – Lower
   Carboniferous
Width 2–3·5 cm

Cyrtospirifer is a member of the very important group of brachiopods called the Spiriferida which are used as zone fossils for the Devonian period. It is strongly biconvex with the hinge line equal to the maximum width of the shell. The beak of the pedicle valve is very strong and curves over the large interarea. A notch for the passage of the pedicle is present below the beak. Both valves are ornamented by numerous ridges which are simple on the lateral slopes of the shell but are forked in the pedicle depression and on the brachial fold. The fold and depression in the shell are related to the currents generated by the feeding organ. *C. verneuili* is a well-known species from the Upper Devonian of Europe.

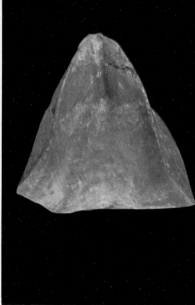

Uncites

Europe, Asia
Middle Devonian
Length 3—4·5 cm

Uncites is a rather specialized spiriferid but, like the majority of this group, it has a spiral support structure for the feeding organ. This structure is only occasionally visible and therefore external characters are of extreme importance. Uncites is biconvex with a very long curved beak. The depression and fold of other spiriferids are missing and the valves are ornamented by forked ribs. These are crossed by growth lines which are irregular in their occurrence. An outstanding feature of Uncites is the size of pedicle notch, which is triangular in shape and dominates the central region of the interarea. U. gryphus is a noted species from the Middle Devonian of Europe; the elongate ventral beak and rather specialized shape making it an easy fossil to identify.

Pugnax

England, Eire
Middle Devonian — Carboniferous
Width 3—4·5 cm

Although Pugnax itself is restricted in its distribution, related forms are known throughout Europe in the Devonian and Carboniferous. In general they are comparatively small with a tetrahedral shape. In Pugnax the depression and fold are broad without strict definition. In some species, such as P. acuminatus, the fold gives the brachial valve a keel-shaped appearance. The pedicle valve is flatter with a tongue-shaped extension in the forward anterior region. Both valves may be heavily ornamented with ribs but this varies with different species and in some the shells are almost smooth. In the posterior region, the beak is small and marked with ridges. The interareas are also small and overhung by the incurved beak.

Syringothyris

Worldwide
Upper Devonian – Carboniferous
Width 4–6 cm

A medium-sized spiriferid in which the shell is strongly biconvex with a deep depression in the pedicle valve. The valves are ornamented by strong ridges on the lateral slopes but the depression and brachial fold are 'bald'. Fine concentric lines indicate the growth of the valves. The pedicle interarea is very large with a conspicuous notch for the passage of the pedicle. The pedicle valve is the larger of the two, with the hinge line being equal to the maximum width of the shell. It is possible that the broad flat interarea was developed to spread the weight of the shell over the soft substrate. The range and wide distribution of *Syringothyris* suggest that it was successful within its own niche.

Spiriferina

Worldwide
Triassic – Lower Jurassic
Width 3–4 cm

A small- to medium-sized spiriferid known mainly from sediments of Lower Jurassic age. The species *S. walcotti* is recorded from the Lias of Europe. The shell is biconvex, having a distinct fold and depression. The lateral slopes on either sides of the fold are often coarsely ribbed. Posteriorly, the pedicle interarea is seen to be very large and slightly overhung by the beak. Apart from the coarse ornament, distinct concentric growth lines are noticeable and in some forms five tubular spines may occur. A study of the shell surface with a hand-lens or microscope would reveal that the shell is pierced by numerous fine pores. The term applied to this type of structure is **punctate**.

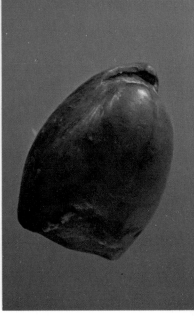

Goniorhynchia

Europe
Middle Jurassic
Width 3—4 cm

Goniorhynchia is a useful fossil to the European stratigrapher. It is a medium-sized rather wide rhynchonellid, a group of brachiopods noted usually for their limited size, coarse ribbing, and prominent pointed beaks. In *Goniorhynchia* the shell is characterized by a single strong upfold of the pedicle valve which is mirrored in the front line of the brachial one. The shell is coarsely ribbed back to the beak area, but the beak itself is small and slightly curved. The hinge line is short and rounded with several strong teeth visible when one discovers separated valves. Other well-known Jurassic forms such as *Gibbirhynchia* and *Tetrarhynchia* belong to the same family as *Goniorhynchia*.

Digonella

Europe
Middle Jurassic
Width 2—4 cm

Digonella is a terebratulid brachiopod, and like other members of the order, it has a smooth shell with a well-developed beak area on the pedicle valve and a circular opening for the pedicle. Many terebratulids are also tear-drop shaped, but *Digonella* has a rather square anterior margin. It is a small- to medium-sized brachiopod which is generally biconvex. The hinge line is rounded, the greatest width of the shell being across the squared anterior area. Internally, *Digonella* has a looped support structure similar to many other terebratulids. Traces of a midline septum are often seen on the weathered surface of the brachial valve. Concentric growth lines ornament both valves.

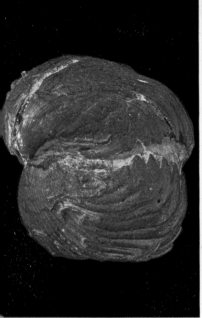

Rhactorhynchia

Worldwide
Jurassic
Width 2–4 cm

Rhactorhynchia is a medium- to large-sized rhynchonellid with a rounded swollen appearance. Both valves are convex with an ornament of numerous sharp ridges or ribs. The pedicle valve has a strong beak that is slightly incurved towards the brachial valve. A small pedicle foramen is present and careful study shows that it occurs below the ridges that mark the line of the beak. In the front of the shell, the commissure is marked by the presence of a feeble often asymmetrical fold. The character of this fold was obviously significant in naming the species *R. inconstans*. At its most prolific, *Rhactorhynchia* was known from the south Asian area to Europe, Africa, and North America.

Sellithyris

Europe
Cretaceous
Width 1–3 cm

The terebratulid, *Sellithyris*, is known from England, France, Belgium, Germany, and Switzerland. It is small to medium in size with a flattened but biconvex shell. The surfaces of the valves are smooth, marked only by strong concentric growth lines. Anteriorly, the **commissure** has two distinct folds which vary in prominence with growth; young individuals often lack any sign of folding. Posteriorly, the rounded opening for the pedicle is large and clearly defined. The beak is usually described as pointing upwards. Internally, the support structure for the feeding organ is short and broad in character. In some localities *Sellithyris* is found in 'nests' where hundreds of individuals are found packed together in a depression on the ancient sea-floor.

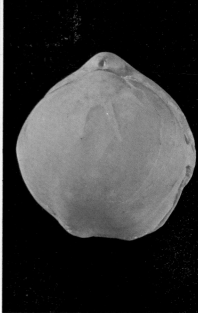

Dereta

Europe
Upper Cretaceous
Length 1·5—3 cm

Dereta is a small- to large-sized tere-bratulid in which the shell is strongly biconvex. The two valves are thick and marked by strong external radiating ribs. The opening between the valves, the commissure, is gently downfolded and has a crenulate appearance. The beak is gently curved towards the brachial valve and the lateral areas, below and to the side of the beak, are smooth. A large pedicle opening is present with a well-defined pedical collar. Apart from the radial ribbing, pronounced concentric growth lines mark the shell surface. Internally, there is a thick septum and a distinct support loop. The pedical opening is round to oval in appearance and comparatively large for the size of the shell. *D. tectita* is a well-known form from the Upper Cretaceous of England.

Gibbithyris

Europe
Upper Cretaceous
Width 1·5—2·5 cm

The shell of *Gibbithyris* is small to medium in size. Both valves are strongly convex, lacking ribs but ornamented with well-developed concentric growth lines. The pedicle valve is much the larger of the two with the umbo incurved, to rest against the posterior brachial area. The pedicle opening although small is clearly defined. Anteriorly, the commissure is either straight or gently folded, while a forward view of the shell gives a rather swollen image. The hinge line of *Gibbithyris* is short and rounded and characterized by the presence of small teeth and narrow sockets. Internally, the brachial support or loop is short measuring only one-third of the brachial valve's total length. The presence of several species suggests that *Gibbithyris* was a successful terebratulid.

Mollusca

The molluscs are probably the most important of the invertebrate phyla. They are thought to have originated in the late Precambrian and have, through time, occupied a wide variety of marine, freshwater, and terrestrial niches. The variety of forms is apparently boundless with snails, clams, squids, tusk shells, and chitons being recent representatives of ancient stocks. In the fossil record, the nautiloids, ammonoids, and belemnites added to the variety of the phylum.

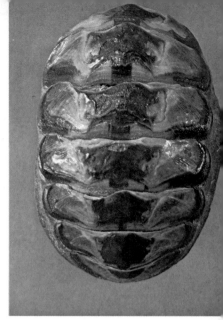

Chitons (Amphineura)

Worldwide
Ordovician — Recent
Length 1–30 cm

The chitons are probably the least well known of the various classes of Mollusca. They are characterized by an outer skeleton consisting of eight 'valves' which are surrounded by a narrow girdle structure. In living forms, innumerable calcareous spines or spicules occur over the girdle but these have yet to be found fossilized. The front and rear valves are narrower yet longer than the intermediate ones. In living forms, the valves overlap each other to give an imbricate structure; this is also characteristic of most Mesozoic and Cainozoic forms, while the valves of those recorded from the Palaeozoic tend to abut against each other. One hundred or more species of chiton have been described from the fossil record, the majority of discoveries consisting of isolated valves. *Gryphochiton priscus* is a well-known species from the Lower Carboniferous of Belgium.

Tentaculites

Worldwide
Ordovician — Devonian
Length 0·5–2 cm

During the Palaeozoic a number of fossils occur that defy direct association with any living organism. The conodonts are included in this description, and so is *Tentaculites* and a number of supposedly related genera. The skeleton of *Tentaculites* is calcareous and has the form of an elongate cone. It has a circular cross-section and the apical area is closed or solid. The shell is either straight or slightly curved and the external surface is distinguished by a pattern of transverse parallel rings. This type of shell bears comparison with those of fossils associated with the worms and gastropods, and as yet no real decision has been made on their classification. In some localities, many thousands of tentaculid shells can be discovered on one small bedding plane exposure.

Hyolithes

Europe, North America
Lower Cambrian — Lower Permian
Length 1–2 cm

Like *Tentaculites*, *Hyolithes* is a fossil of doubtful association, although various authors have linked it firmly with the gastropods. It has a straight calcareous shell with a pyramidal form. In cross-section, the shell varies from triangular to nearly circular; the aperture being covered by an operculum. In some forms the external surface is smooth but in others it is marked with fine striations. The shell of *Hyolithes* is normally hollow, but septal divisions have been recorded from the initial growth area of some specimens. As with *Tentaculites*, the shells of *Hyolithes* are often found in great abundance at certain outcrops. The case for associating *Hyolithes* with the gastropods is based on the discovery of a single specimen with wing-like extensions similar to those of the living pteropods.

Gastropoda

The gastropods represent one of the main divisions of Mollusca. They include both the snails and slugs; the former having a geological record dating from the Cambrian period. They bear coiled or uncoiled calcareous shells, the shape and ornament of which are used in classification. Uncoiled shells are usually cone-like or cap-shaped with an excentric apical area. Coiled shells are more variable, however, with **planispiral** and **conispiral** types predominant. One complete loop of a shell is termed a **whorl**, the **body-whorl** being the last and largest to be formed. All whorls above this last, are collectively known as the **spire**. In most forms a distinct spiral **suture**, separates the whorls. A solid or perforate central pillar, the **columella**, is found in conispiral shells. Where the columella emerges, it forms part of the inner lip of the **aperture**. The aperture itself may be rounded or may have an elongate appearance with anterior and posterior **notches** present.

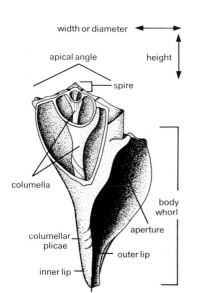

Pleurotomaria

Worldwide
Lower Jurassic – Lower Cretaceous
Diameter 5–7 cm

Pleurotomaria belongs to an ancient order of gastropods which ranges from the late Cambrian to the present day. It has a conical spiral shell in which the spiral angle is quite wide. The whorls of the shell increase gradually so that sides are fairly even, up to and including the body whorl. This last whorl has a somewhat flattened base and an aperture that is rather square in outline. A prominant slit occurs on the outer lip which, as the shell grew, was filled to form a slit band or **selenizone**. The growth lines on the whorls are directed obliquely backwards towards the slit band and small nodes may ornament the upper and lower whorl margins. *Pleurotomaria* is particularly well known from Jurassic sediments.

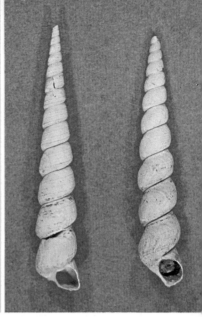

Calliostoma

Worldwide
Cretaceous – Recent
Length 1–4 cm

Calliostoma has a conical shell with a spire of intermediate height. The spire is also straight sided with a sharp to moderate spiral angle. In some species the suture lines are clearly marked but in others they are relatively indistinct. The aperture of *Calliostoma* is rounded to subrounded lacking both a siphonal notch and slit. There is slight thickening of the inner lip and no umbilicus is present in this genus. The ornament consists of spiral ridges, the strength and distribution of which vary with the species. In *C. schlueteri* (Cretaceous) for example, a pronounced ridge is present on the shoulder of each whorl, while in *C. subexcavatum* (Lower Pleistocene) several pitted ridges have equal strength and an evenly-spaced distribution.

Turritella

Worldwide
Oligocene – Recent
Length 3–8 cm

As its name suggests, *Turritella* has a very long turreted spire which forms a very acute apical angle. The spire is formed of many whorls, the side walls of which are either flat or slightly rounded. The body whorl is only a little larger than the one before and the aperture is rounded and entire. In most species the outer lip is thin and slightly sinuous. The whorls are usually ornamented with spiral ribs and the normal growth striations. Numerous species of *Turritella* flourished during the Tertiary and although many species at first appear identical, a careful study of ornament and whorl shape enables an accurate identification to be made. In some localities, the shells of *Turritella* may exhibit a distinct orientation related to the water currents that existed prior to burial.

Rimella

Worldwide
Eocene — Recent
Length 1–3·5 cm

Rimella is a very distinct gastropod in which the shell is fusiform and the spire elongate. The spire is formed of many whorls and is characterized by the adherence of a posterior canal, which extends almost from the aperture to the apex of the shell. The whorls are gently rounded and show a gradual increase from spire to body whorl, although the latter is much larger than those that preceded it. In *Rimella*, the aperture is very narrow with the long posterior canal noted above together with a shorter anterior one. Both lips are thickened, with the inner one expanded to overlap the body whorl. The ornament of *Rimella* consists of strong vertical ribs and spiral striations, which together give a cancellate patterning. *R. rimosa* is found in relative abundance in the Lutetian (Middle Eocene) of Northwest Europe.

Aporrhais

Worldwide
Jurassic — Recent
Length 4–8 cm

The shell of *Aporrhais* is turretted with a large flared, often spinose, wing which may extend from the spire to the tip of the siphonal canal. The apical angle is narrow and the rounded whorls exhibit a uniform decrease in size towards the apex. Each suture is clearly defined with the faces of the two whorls inturned towards the axis. This type of suture, which gives the rounded effect noted above, is termed **impressed**. A bold sculpture of vertical ridges and tubercules occurs on each whorl, while fine growth lines can be distinguished on the flared outer lip (wing). In life, *Aporrhais* is a shallow burrower which obtains its food from the mud in which it lives, and is now restricted to the North Atlantic.

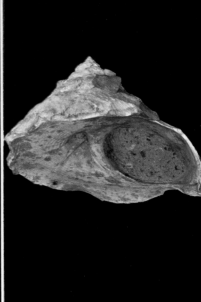

Clavilithes

Europe, North America, Asia
Eocene — Pliocene
Adult length 10–15 cm

The shell of *Clavilithes* is robust in construction and fusiform or spindle-shaped in form, tapering gradually towards both ends. Each whorl is clearly distinguished by a deeply impressed suture and a prominent shoulder area. The whorls decrease uniformly to the apex, which in the species *C. rugosus* is strongly ornamented. In other species, the apex, like the remainder of the shell, is relatively smooth with a fine ornament of growth lines and spiral striations. The spire of *Clavilithes* is quite long and the apical angle moderate. The walls of the body whorl and other whorls are almost vertical. The aperture is **siphonostomatous**, the siphonal canal being long and narrow. Internally, the columella is stout and lacks the plications typical of many genera.

Xenophora

Worldwide
Cretaceous — Recent
Width 5–8 cm

Xenophora has a low conical shell in which the base is flattened or slightly concave. In dorsal view, the shell is distinctly spiral in form with the body whorl having a sharp outer margin. A large aperture occurs on the underside, and is obliquely positioned. A wide and rather deep umbilicus is also characteristic of the lower surface, although in some specimens it may be partially covered by a thick callus. Several species of *Xenophora* have a highly sculptured surface, but others may be fairly smooth or covered with fragments of shell or rock debris. *X. agglutinans* from the Middle Eocene is typical of this last type, the name being derived from its habit of sticking fragments to the shell surface (agglutination).

Natica

Worldwide
Triassic — Recent
Height 1–5 cm

The shape of *Natica* varies from globular to conical. The shell is medium sized and invariably smooth with faint growth lines. In most species the spire is very short with the enormous body whorl forming the greater part of the shell. The walls of the individual whorls are gently rounded and distinct shoulders occur in most species. *Natica* has a subrounded entire aperture with a thin outer lip and a thickened inner one. A distinct callus occurs on the columella and in some individuals it may cover the umbilicus. Numerous species of *Natica* flourished during the Eocene of Europe, with small borings in the shells of other molluscs revealing the predatory habits of this genus.

Planorbis

Europe, Africa, Asia
Upper Jurassic — Recent
Width 0·5–5 cm

Planorbis is a small- to medium-sized gastropod which inhabits freshwater environments. The shell is strong walled, forming a spirally coiled flattened disc. In *P. planorbis* the upper surface of the shell is flattened while the lower surface is characterized by the convex nature of each whorl. The shell is coiled in a single plane (planispiral) with whorls showing a gradual increase towards the body whorl. On the lower surface the sutures are of an impressed variety. The aperture varies with the species and may be oval, widely cresentic, or rhomboidal in outline. Fine growth lines mark the outer surface of what otherwise would be described as a smooth shell. The umbilicus of *Planorbis* is deep and the spire low to slightly sunken.

Poleumita

Europe, North America
Lower Silurian
Width 4–9 cm

The shape of *Poleumita* like that of *Straparollus* (*Euomphalus*, Silurian – Middle Permian, worldwide) is sub-discoidal. The spire ranges from depressed to slightly elevated with deep sutures indicating the outline of the whorls. Unlike *Straparollus* (*Euomphalus*), the upper whorl surfaces of *Poleumita* bear two types of plate-like markings which follow the outline of the lip. The upper surface is also characterized by the presence of a raised angular ridge. In some species, slightly raised spines may occur on the shoulder of each whorl. The umbilicus, the depression formed around the axis of the shell, is broad. In *Poleumita* the early parts of the shell are abandoned and sealed off by septa.

Straparollus (Euomphalus)

Worldwide
Silurian – Middle Permian
Diameter 3–4 cm

Euomphalus was the name formerly given to *Straparollus* and was the name on which the well-known family *Euomphalidae* was founded. (*Poleumita* is also a member of this family.) The shell of *Straparollus* is subdiscoidal in shape, with a depressed spire and a wide umbilicus. An angular ridge is present on the outer upper edge of the whorl, with a channel occurring on the inner surface. The lower surfaces of the whorls may be angular or rounded in form. Fine growth lines are present around the whorls, paralleling the out-line of the outer lip. Spiral threads or a row of nodes may also form part of the ornament. Some species of *Straparollus* may have a moderately high conispiral shell.

Sycostoma (Sycum)

Worldwide
Eocene
Length 3–6 cm

Sycostoma has a bulbous shell in which the body whorl is greatly inflated. The spire is short with a narrow apex but the whorls expand rapidly towards the body chamber. Distinct suture lines occur on the spire. Below the final suture, the upper part of the body whorl is somewhat flattened before the curve of the side walls. The aperture is relatively narrow with an elongate straight siphonal canal. *Sycostoma* has a curved outer apertural lip and a smooth inner one which often has a shiny polished appearance. Apart from a series of spiral lines, which arise from the area of the columellar lip in some species, the shell of *Sycostoma* has a smooth surface. *S. bulbiformis* is a representative species from the Lutetian (Middle Eocene) stage.

Neptunea (Chrysodomus)

Worldwide
Eocene – Recent
Length 6–12 cm

The shell of *Neptunea* is robust in character. It has a fusiform shape, with an elongate spire and a pronounced but short siphonal canal. The whorls are rounded with a sloping shoulder and an indented suture. In all species the body whorl is very large accounting for over half the size of the shell. The aperture is oval with a simple outer lip and a slightly thickened but smooth inner one. *Neptunea* exhibits both dextral (aperture on right-hand side) and sinistral (aperture on left-hand side) coiling, with the latter being the least common. The external ornament varies from smooth to strongly ridged. *N. contraria* and *N. despecta decemcostata* are well-known Quaternary species. The first has a smooth ornament while the second has spiral ridging.

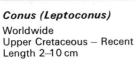

Conus (Leptoconus)

Worldwide
Upper Cretaceous – Recent
Length 2–10 cm

Conus is a conical gastropod with a flat or shallow spire. The body whorl is very large and the aperture is elongate and narrow. The borders of the aperture are parallel with the outer lip, which is simple in form. A well-defined notch occurs at the upper end of the aperture while the lower region ends in a short canal. The columella of *Conus* is straight and without the plications found in other genera. Spiral grooves, ridges, and tubercules may occur as the external ornament in different species. The spire may have a large number of whorls and spiral ridges ornament this area of the shell. Several well-known species previously referred to *Conus* are now included in the genus *Leptoconus.*

Fusinus (Fusus)

Worldwide
Cretaceous – Recent
Length 3–6 cm

Fusinus, because of its exceptionally long and narrow siphonal canal, is a very well-known gastropod. The shell is also rather long and narrow with a prominent spire made up of a large number of rounded whorls. *Fusinus* has a fusiform shape, tapering sharply towards both ends. The aperture is rounded with a thin uncomplicated outer lip, which in some species is marked by fine ridges on the inner surface. The columella is smooth without any folds. On the external surface, the ornament of the various species referred to *Fusinus* differs considerably, with transverse and spiral ribs forming complex and varied patterns. These and the number of whorls included in the spire are important characters in the classification of this genus:

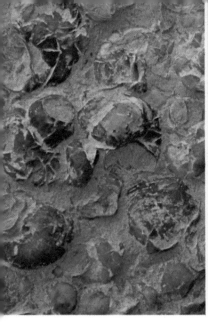

Viviparus

Worldwide
Jurassic — Recent
Diameter 1·5—3 cm

Viviparus is a small- to medium-sized gastropod, with a broadly conical spire and a convex base. In the majority of specimens, the whorls are smooth and convex but some species have been described as possessing carinate whorls. This means that a prominent spiral ridge or keel is present on the whorls. Other species are characterized by the presence of knot-like protuberances. Today, species of *Viviparus* live in freshwater environments and the young emerge from the ovum within the parent (viviparous). It is likely that fossil species had similar lifestyles and are therefore valuable in the identification of freshwater sediments. The geological record of *Viviparus* may be extended to the Lower Carboniferous if the identification of a single internal mould ever obtains acceptance.

Capulus

Worldwide
Ordovician — Recent
Diameter 2—3 cm

As its name suggests, the shell of *Capulus* is cap-shaped with a large rounded to irregular aperture. The shell is thin and curves upwards and backwards to the apex. In some individuals, the apex markedly overhangs the rear of the shell and sometimes exhibits a spiral inrolling. The ornament of *Capulus* varies with the species, although fine radial ribs are most common. Internally, the shell is usually smooth except for the occurrence of a large horseshoe-shaped muscle scar in the posterior position. *Capulus* is relatively abundant in Palaeozoic rocks but is of more limited importance in Mesozoic and Cainozoic deposits. It is a bottom-dwelling gastropod feeding on detritus.

Hippochrenes

Europe, Asia
Eocene
Length 12–25 cm

Hippochrenes is a medium- to large-sized gastropod with a fusiform shell which supports an expanded outer lip. The spire is long and tapering, with the sutures being almost flush with the shell surface. *Hippochrenes* has a narrow apical angle and the expansion of the shell, into and including the body whorl, is very gradual. The lower region of the body whorl is extended to form a siphonal canal which is deflected slightly towards the inner surface of the outer lip. The latter, as stated above, is greatly expanded or flared to form a wing that extends from the lower whorl of the spire to halfway down the siphonal tube. Unlike the wing of *Aporrhais*, that of *Hippochrenes* is rounded and without spines. The shell surface is smooth.

Athleta (Voluta)

North America, Europe, Africa, Asia
Eocene – Recent
Length 2–10 cm

A thick-shelled gastropod which has a short spire and turban-like protoconch. The body whorl is very large with an elongate siphonostomatous aperture. Strong nodes or vertical spines occur along the shoulder of the body whorl and these are continued over the surface of the whorl as transverse ribs. These are also present on the whorls of the spire, where growth lines add further to the external ornament. The aperture is also narrow with a thick outer lip, and an inner lip which has a thin callus. In most species, the upper end of the aperture is characterized by the presence of an angular channel, while the lower region is deeply notched. Several plications occur around the base of the columella.

Bivalvia

Known also as the Pelecypoda or Lamellibranchia, these invertebrates are characterized by a shell comprising two valves which are usually mirror images of each other (**equivalve**). However, some forms such as the rudistids and oysters may be strongly **inequivalve**. A **hinge line** is readily distinguished with **hinge teeth** and **sockets** being present in many individuals. The form of the teeth and their arrangement on the hinge line are used in the classification of the group. Each valve has a **beak** which in the vast majority of cases points anteriorly. The flattened area in front of the beak is termed the **lunule**, and the one behind, the **escutcheon**. Both valves may have an external ornament of concentric **growth lines** and or radial **ribs**. Internally, a **pallial line** marks the inner margin of the thickened mantle edges; an inward inflection at the posterior of this line marking the position of the siphons.

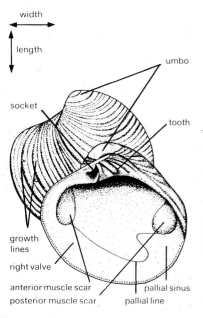

Nucula

Worldwide
Upper Cretaceous — Recent
Width 1–3 cm

Like *Acila*, *Nucula* is a member of the subclass Palaeotaxodonta. The shell consists of two equal valves in which the anterior and posterior areas are of equal length (equilateral). No gape occurs between the valve margins. The beaks of *Nucula* point posteriorly, this condition being described as **opisthogyrous**. Externally, the shell may have a polished appearance or a fine sculpture of radiating ribs. Numerous subequal teeth occur along the hinge line; the internal surface of the shell often has a lustrous mother-of-pearl appearance. The muscle scars of *Nucula* are of equal size (isomyarian) and the pallial line is entire along its length. *Nucula* is a shallow burrowing bivalve, its rather rounded shell differing from the more streamlined elongate form of deeper-burrowing individuals.

59

Acila

Europe, Americas, North Africa,
  Japan, Asia
Lower Cretaceous — Recent
Width 1·5–3 cm

As with closely related genera, *Acila*
and *Nucula* have many features in
common. Both belong to the family
Nuculidae which in turn is referred to
the subclass Palaeotaxodonta. The
shells of *Acila* may be quadrangular to
ovate in outline, while the shell ornament consists of widely spaced
concentric growth lines and pairs of
faint ridges that diverge from the midline; the total effect is diagnostic of the
genus. Numerous subequal teeth occur
along the hinge line and the **resilifer**, a
small process for the attachment of the
internal ligament, occurs below the
beak. The muscle scars are of equal
size (isomyarian) and the pallial line is
entire. Like the majority of genera referred to the family Nuculidae, *Acila* is
a shallow-burrowing bivalve which
feeds on detritus.

Parallelodon

Worldwide
Lower Ordovician — Upper Jurassic
Width 7–12 cm

The shell of *Parallelodon* is more than
twice as long as it is high. It is also
strongly biconvex, with the valves
being of roughly equal size and strongly
inequilateral. The umbones are placed
anteriorly but are broad and occupy
nearly a quarter of the shell length. In
some species, the posterior region is
wing-like and is clearly defined from
the rest of the shell. The external ornament is made up of radial ribs and
irregularly occurring growth lines. In
Parallelodon, the hinge line is long and
straight with a characteristic dentition
of several elongate posterior laterals
and numerous oblique anterior cardinals. The genus is similar in many ways
to *Arca*, although any direct link with
the living genus is unlikely.

Modiolus (Modiola)

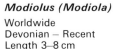

Worldwide
Devonian — Recent
Length 3–8 cm

The term **modioliform** is used to describe the shell of *Modiolus* and others like it. Essentially, the term relates to rather elongate shells in which the beaks occur slightly behind the anterior end and where the forward lower portion forms a noticeable bulge. The external ornament lacks radial ribs but concentric growth lines form a distinctive pattern. *Modiolus* has poorly developed hinge teeth and the muscle scars are of unequal size (anisomyarian); the anterior scar is much smaller. Recent species are free-living with individuals adopting a nestling habit. In modern-day forms, the outer horny periostracum that covers the calcareous shell is hairy. This covering is rarely found fossilized.

Lithophaga

Worldwide
? Carboniferous — Recent
Length 2–3 cm

Unlike the majority of bivalves described in this text, *Lithophaga* is a borer; the animal excavates a cylindrical burrow in rock by means of a chemical solution. The secreted mucous actually dissolves the carbonate rock around the base of the shell; the latter being protected by a thickened periostracum. To conform with this mode of life, the shell of *Lithophaga* is elongate and cylindrical and tapered towards the posterior end. The beaks occur near the anterior end, and the external ornament varies from smooth to lightly striated. Internally, the muscle scars are of different sizes (anisomyarian) while the pallial line is entire. As the burrow increases in width downwards and the shell grows within the enlarged cavity, it becomes impossible for *Lithophaga* to evacuate its permanent home.

Inoceramus

Worldwide
Lower Jurassic — Upper Cretaceous
Length 5–15 cm

The various species referred to the genus *Inoceramus* represent a variety of different shapes and sizes. In the majority, the shells are strongly unequivalve, but in some the difference between the valves, in terms of size, is quite small. To describe the shells of *Inoceramus*, palaeontologists use the words ovate, trapeziform, or suborbicular, that is egg shaped, subrounded, or straight sided with only two of the sides being parallel. The shells may often be extremely large with a layered appearance. In some species, an expanded back wing may be present, while numerous ligamented pits are characteristic of the hinge line. *Inoceramus* has no hinge teeth. The external ornament consists of rather coarse concentric ripples and fine concentric growth lines.

Gervillella

Worldwide
Triassic — Cretaceous
Length 5–20 cm

Gervillella is a medium- to large-sized bivalve. The valves are very long with a very oblique outline, in which the posterior is lengthened and the anterior portion shortened and very pointed. Both valves have an ornament of broad concentric growth lines. *Gervillella* has poorly developed hinge teeth, while the ligament area is long and narrow with a number of pits. The latter mark the areas of attachment of fibrous ligaments. *Gervillella* bears some resemblance to *Mytilus*, the common mussel, to which it is closely related. It is probable that like *Mytilus*, *Gervillella* was a bottom dweller and was fixed rather than active. Several species are found in the Mesozoic rocks of Europe.

Plagiostoma (Lima)

Worldwide
Middle Triassic — Upper Cretaceous
Adult length 10–15 cm

This is a medium- to large-sized bivalve in which the shell is equivalve and inequilateral. The margins of the valves are well rounded while the hinge area is angular with a small ear-like extension anteriorly. In most forms the shell is moderately inflated and slightly longer than it is high. The external surface is usually smooth although radial lines and even weak ribs may occur in some species. A large ligament pit characterizes the hinge line which normally lacks hinge teeth. A single large muscle scar is present in the centre of each valve (monomyarian), although in many individuals these are rather weakly defined. Recent forms related to Plagiostoma swim by flapping their valves. Plagiostoma is relatively abundant in the shallow-water limestones of the Lower Jurassic.

Arca

Worldwide
Middle Jurassic — Recent
Length 2–7 cm

Various species of Arca are known from rocks that span the last 190 million years of geological time. In general, the individuals referred to Arca are medium-sized bivalves. The valves are elongate and convex with the beak, which points slightly forward, placed anterior to the midline. The beaks of each valve are separated by wide flattened areas which are marked by V-shaped grooves. Numerous small comb-like teeth line the elongate hinge line. In the species A. biangula (Eocene) a wide gape is found between the two valves. Both valves are ornamented by radial ribs which are cut by concentric growth lines.

Pinna

Worldwide
Lower Carboniferous — Recent
Length 8–20 cm

Pinna is a bivalve of medium to large size having a rather triangular tooth-shaped appearance. The valves are of equal size, tapering sharply towards the anterior. Externally, the valves may either have a concentric ornament or one composed of long ridges. In the elongate species *P. lanceolata* from the Jurassic, broad concentric growth lines predominate, but radiating ridges characterize part of the anterior region. Posteriorly, the valves are subrounded and separated to form a wide gape. In *Pinna*, the teeth and sockets are reduced to insignificance and the ligament is narrow and external. In life, *Pinna* lived buried in the sediments of the sea-floor, anchored by a large thread-like byssus.

Glycimeris

Worldwide
Lower Cretaceous — Recent
Width 1·5–5 cm

Like *Arca*, *Mytilus*, *Pecten*, and numerous other well-known genera, *Glycimeris* is included in the subclass Pteriomorpha. The various stocks referred to this subclass live mainly in a fixed position on the seabed, but a few genera are secondarily free. Adult glycimerids are free, lacking the hair-like byssal attachment associated with the mussels. The shell of *Glycimeris* is subcircular in outline with the vertical beaks directed towards the opposite valve (orthogyrate). Externally the shell is usually rather smooth, marked only by fine concentric growth lines. In a few species, however, radial ribbing does occur. Internally, the cardinal area is noted for the presence of one or more chevron grooves, while the hinge line is characterized by a large number of strong taxodont teeth. The pallial line is entire in this genus and the muscle scars are of roughly equal size (isomyarian).

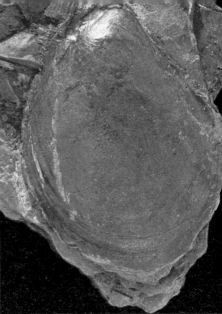

Pecten

Worldwide
Upper Eocene – Recent
Width 2·5–10 cm

A small- to medium-sized bivalve in which the valves are of unequal size; the right valve is more convex than the left. As a scallop, Pecten has a rounded outline except for anterior and posterior wings which occur along the hinge line. The anterior and posterior halves of the valves are almost symmetrical in shape. Strong radially arranged folds or **plications** mark the external surface, and the leading edge of the shell has a serrated appearance. In some species, concentric growth lines may also form part of the ornament. *Pecten* lacks any signs of teeth and sockets but a well-developed triangular ligament notch is common to both valves. A large single muscle scar is also typical of both valves of this genus. The modern *Pecten* is able to swim freely by a 'flapping' action of the valves.

Modiolopsis

Worldwide
Middle – Upper Ordovician
Width 3–5 cm

Modiolopsis is a member of the extinct Palaeozoic order Modiomorphoida. In the main, these bivalves have rather elongate shells in which both valves are of equal size. The valves are often expanded posteriorly and apart from well-defined concentric growth lines lack any ornamentation. In *Modiolopsis*, the valves are more rounded than many of the genera referred to the order and lack hinge teeth. The beaks are low and in life the ligament was sited behind the beak area. Internally, the muscle scars are of different sizes (**anisomyarian**) with the posterior scar being slightly the larger of the two. In many ways *Modiolopsis* and related genera resemble the common mussel, and it is possible that a member of the order Modiomorphoida was the ancestral form.

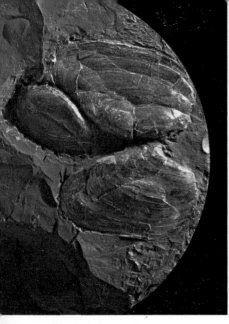

Anthraconauta

Worldwide
Upper Carboniferous — Permian
Length 2—3 cm

Anthraconauta is an important non-marine member of the Myalinidae. The shell is equivalve, inequilateral in form, with a straight hinge line and rather inconspicuous umbones. In the majority of individuals the hinge line accounts for between half to three quarters of the length and forms an obtuse angle with the shell's straight or slightly curved posterior margin. The shell is rather thin with an ornament of pronounced concentric growth lines. In some forms folds may characterize the ornament and the surface may have a rough texture. Radial lines of a rather delicate nature are known for a few species. The internal characteristics of *Anthraconauta* are as yet unknown. Identification of carboniferous freshwater mussels is often problematic due to similarity of shell form.

Carbonicola

Western Europe, USSR
Carboniferous, particularly Upper
    Carboniferous
Width 3—5 cm

Several species of *Carbonicola*, including *C. communis* and *C. pseudo-robusta*, are important in the stratigraphic correlation of the Upper Carboniferous coal measures. Both species are diagnostic of the **communis** zone. As in *Anthraconauta*, the shell of *Carbonicola* is elongate and inequilateral and the hinge line is slightly curved, but the umbones are erect and of slightly unequal height. In well-preserved specimens, the external ornament is seen to be stronger towards the margin, whereas in *Anthraconauta* the concentric growth lines cover the whole surface. Both shells and moulds of *Carbonicola* appear inflated; the lunule and escutcheon areas being well defined. Nonmarine bivalves inhabited the swampy environments of the Upper Carboniferous, often grouped together to form 'mussel bands'.

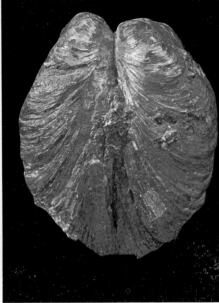

Trigonia

Worldwide
Middle Triassic — Upper Cretaceous
Width 4—8 cm

As the name suggests, *Trigonia* has an almost triangular form with the anterior portion being much shortened. The valves are of equal size and the beak is directed upwards and slightly backwards. The surface markings are distinctive, with either concentric ridges or nodose radially directed ribs, or a combination of both. Frequently the concentric ridges ornament the anterior of the shell, while other markings cover posterior areas. This variety of markings enables a rapid determination at species level. The escutcheon, found along the hinge line behind the beak, is also a characteristic of the trigonids. Internally, two prominent teeth with grooved surfaces occur on the hinge line of the right valve.

Hippopodium

Europe, East Africa
Jurassic
Width 5—8 cm

This large bivalve is the type and only genus of the family Hippopodiidae. It has a thick kidney-shaped shell in which the beaks are placed and directed anteriorly and the valve margins have a layered appearance. Both valves appear inflated ·with the beaks being well separated in adult specimens. The external ornament of the shell consists of irregularly arranged and strongly developed growth lines. Internally, the hinge line is curved with a modified dentition of two broad cardinal teeth (one in each valve) and a posterior lateral tooth in the right valve. The muscle scars are of slightly different sizes (**anisomyarian**) and the pallial line is entire. *H. ponderosum* is abundant in the Lower Jurassic of Northwest Europe.

Astarte

Worldwide
Jurassic — Recent
Width 2–5 cm

Astarte is closely related to *Crassatella* and the shells of both bivalves are described as trigonal to subtrapezoidal in outline. Both are heterodont bivalves, the diagnostic feature of which is the differentiation of the hinge teeth into midline cardinals and laterals. The shell of *Astarte* is characterized by the presence of a small beak and an external ornament which consists of a number of regularly spaced concentric ribs. The cardinal teeth are well developed on the hinge line. Internally, one notices that the muscle scars are of equal size (**isomyarian**) and that the pallial line is entire. In some species the margin of each valve is marked on the inner surface by short closely spaced grooves, which gives the margin a denticulate appearance.

Hippurites

Europe, Africa, North America, Asia
Upper Cretaceous
Length 12–25 cm

Hippurites is a member of a specialized group of bivalves commonly termed rudists. They are inequivalve with the right valve large and rather coral-like in appearance. The left valve is flattened or slightly convex with a somewhat lid-like character. When first described, *Hippurites* was referred to as a 'horn', the reference being attributed to the local people of southern France who obviously appreciated the cylindrical nature of the right valve. The articulation between the valves is facilitated by the presence of two teeth and a socket in the left valve, and two sockets and one tooth in the right valve. The wall of the right valve is relatively thick and rather cellular in character. The rudists were adapted to life in reef and shallow-shelf environments.

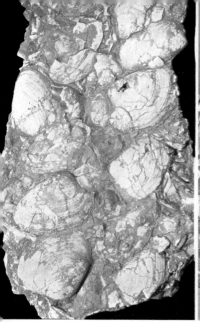

Corbula

Worldwide
Cretaceous – Recent
Width 8–25 cm

The shell of *Corbula* is sturdily built, with the two valves being inequilateral and slightly inequivalve. In all species the right valve is the larger, although the difference in size is often very slight. Both valves are rostrate, the posterior area tapering and curving quite sharply. In *Corbula* itself, the external sculpture consists of a strong concentric ribbing, but in closely related genera such as *Corbula* (*Bicorbula*) the ornament is smooth. No lunule or escutcheon areas occur in this genus. On the internal surfaces, the hinge lines appear to be slightly overhung by the umbones which are directed posteriorly. The hinge lines are characterized by the presence of a posterior cardinal tooth and a ligament pit on the left valve and a posterior lateral tooth on the right. The muscle scars are subequal in size and the pallial line is entire.

Teredo

Worldwide (Recent)
Eocene – Recent
Tube diameter 8–12 mm

Although cosmopolitan in its distribution at present, *Teredo* was for much of its geological record confined to Western Europe. Like *Lithophaga*, *Teredo* is a borer, but its medium is wood and it excavates by grinding away the surrounding material. Although the actual burrow provides protection for the animal, *Teredo* also secretes secondary calcareous tubes to maximize the permanency of its shelter. In many fossil discoveries these tubes are the only record of the bivalve's activity. The shell itself is much reduced, covering only the anterior portion of a very long animal. Externally, the ornament of the shell is divided into several zones, with the most anterior one being characterized by short strong spines which are used during the boring process.

Crassatella

Europe, North America
Middle Cretaceous — Miocene
Width 2·5–5 cm

The shell of *Crassatella* is usually described as subtrapezoidal, although other genera referred to the same family may have a trigonal outline. Both valves are ornamented by concentric ribs, which exhibit posterior angulation. The shell of *Crassatella* is rather thick and the beaks are directed anteriorly (**prosogyrous**). To the front and rear of the beaks, the lunule and escutcheon are characteristically deep. Internally, the hinge area is noted for the presence of the internal ligament pit and the cardinal and lateral teeth. The muscle scars are rather broad and **isomyarian**, being linked by a well-defined pallial line which is entire along its length. The inner margins of the valves are marked by fine crenulations.

Venericor

Europe, North America
Palaeocene — Eocene
Width 3–12 cm

As a member of the superfamily Carditacea, the rounded trigonal shell of *Venericor* has a strong external ornament of radial ribs; concentric growth lines occur in a band paralleling the margin. The beaks are strongly developed and point towards the anterior. Along the hinge line the cardinal teeth are very large and all but one are curved. The muscle scars are also large with the posterior one having a rather pear-shaped outline. Below and between the muscle scars the pallial line is entire, while the valve margins are quite deeply notched (crenulate). The exterior ornament of juvenile specimens is more angular than that of adults. The species *V. planicostata* is an important constituent of European Lutetian (Middle Eocene) faunas.

Venus

Europe, Africa, East Indies, North
  America
Oligocene — Recent
Width 1·5—4 cm

Bivalves referred to the genus *Venus*
are characterized by rounded or ovate
shells, in which the beaks point in the
anterior direction. The ornament of the
shells varies with the species, the
recent *V. verrucosa* having a concentric ribbing which is interrupted both
anteriorly and posteriorly by strong
radial ridges. In fossil species, the shell
surface is usually smoother, however,
and concentric growth lines form the
most common type of ornament. Both
the lunule and escutcheon are well
developed in *Venus*, with the latter
being rather large and smooth in character. Three cardinal teeth are present
in each valve, while the lateral teeth
are essentially poorly developed. The
muscle scars are of equal size (**isomyarian**) and a small posterior sinus
occurs along the pallial line.

Pholadomya

Worldwide
Upper Triassic — Recent
Width 4—6 cm

Pholadomya is a medium- to large-
sized bivalve, the shell of which consists of two inflated or strongly convex
valves. The shell has a rather elongate
appearance, and varies from ovate to
subtrigonal in outline. Both valves are
of equal size but the posterior portion
of each is much larger than the anterior; the shell being described as
strongly inequilateral. The greater in-
flation of the valves occurs anteriorly,
while a noticeable gape is present
posteriorly. A strong ornament is characteristic of most species with a radial
ribbing dominating concentric growth
lines. In some species, small swellings
or pustules occur on the radial ribs.
Although Recent forms are known to
live in fairly deep water, Mesozoic
species are thought to have lived in
shallow-water environments.

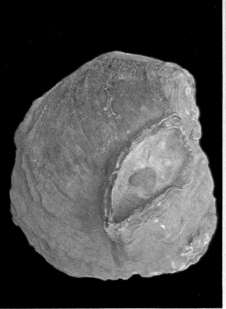

Exogyra

Northern Hemisphere
Cretaceous
Width 8–15 cm

The size of specimens referred to *Exogyra* varies considerably, with the majority of individuals being of medium size. In some ways *Exogyra* strongly resembles *Ostrea*, but the shell is strongly inequivalve with the left valve being much larger than the flat right one. Like *Ostrea* the left valve is orb-shaped or rounded, but the umbonal region is characteristic in being spirally coiled. The ornament of the two valves is variable with concentric growth lines and rounded radiating ribs common in some species. The growth lines, like those of *Ostrea*, often have a layered or foliated appearance. A single large orb-shaped muscle scar is present in the central area of the valves. *Exogyra* lived attached to the substrate.

Gryphea

Worldwide
Upper Triassic – Jurassic
Width 2·5–6 cm

This is frequently referred to as the 'Devil's toenail' due to the form of its two valves, of which the left is much the larger. *Gryphea* is deeply convex with the large beak rolled or curved over onto the right valve. The left valve often has a layered appearance with successive lamellae indicating stages of growth, while the right valve is invariably flat and somewhat rounded, a large muscle scar marks the inner surface. Individual shells grew up to 15 cm in length, the width varying with the species and the mode of life. The very broad shells suggest that some species of *Gryphea* were adapted to live on soft muds.

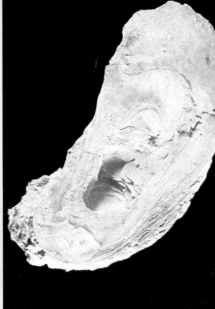

Lopha

Worldwide
Upper Triassic — Recent
Small to medium size length < 11 cm

As with the genus *Ostrea*, *Lopha* is known to incubate its young. Recent species live cemented to the substrate by means of a medium- to large-sized attachment. The valves are not equal in size, although the difference is less than that of many 'oysters'. Both valves are gently convex and have a similar ornament of radiating ribs marked by concentric, somewhat foliate, growth lines. The opening between the valves is strongly folded and has a rather wave-like appearance. In some forms, numerous protuberances and/or claspers may occur which help in fixing the specimen to the substrate. As with other 'oysters', *Lopha* is characterized by the presence of a large single muscle scar on each valve.

Ostrea

Worldwide
Cretaceous — Recent
Largest size, height 18 cm,
  length 20 cm

Since early Mesozoic times, the 'oysters' have ranked among the most successful of bivalve stocks; the general name 'oyster' being applied to a seemingly endless variety of species. In recent years, however, both biological and geological information has been used in the determination and classification of various genera. To this end the genus *Ostrea* is described as incubatory, and lacks an exhalant water passage on the right-hand side of the body. The shell is flat and medium to large in size and generally orb-shaped with a somewhat rounded umbonal region. The gently convex right valve is smaller than the convex left valve, and thin concentric growth lines usually ornament the surface of the former, while the latter is radially ribbed. The ligament areas are triangular in outline and a large rounded muscle scar occurs on both valves.

Cephalopoda

Present-day representatives include the octopoids, sepioids, and nautiloids, while the ammonoids, nautiloids, and belemnoids have important fossil records. All three major fossil stocks have chambered skeletons, but the solid guard of the belemnoids clearly separates them from the other two. The shell of the ammonoids varies from straight to tightly coiled, where the outer **whorls** overlap those inside (involute). Both groups have a tube, the **siphuncle**, which passes through the septa; the position of the siphuncle and the degree of septal folding being extremely important in the classification of individual specimens. In the nautiloids, the siphuncle is dorsal, while it is essentially ventral in the ammonoids. The nautiloids also have straight or slightly curved septa, whereas those of the ammonoids are folded into **lobes** and **saddles**. Distinct changes in the complexity of the lobes and saddles helps to subdivide the Ammonoidea into the goniatites, ceratites, and ammonites.

Nautiloidia
Endoceras
Europe, Asia, North America
Middle — Upper Ordovician
Complete specimen length up to 4 m

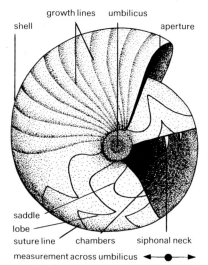

The shell of *Endoceras* is long and straight with a large siphuncle in the ventral position. It has a slightly flattened cross-section and the surface is irregular due to the presence of ring-like expansions of shell (**annulations**). The septa of *Endoceras*, like those of many nautiloids are straight with long septal necks. Secondary deposits of calcite are often found inside the siphuncles of nautiloids and in *Endoceras* they are diagnostic, having the form of a series of backward directed cones. These cones were associated with the buoyancy of the animal, which in other nautiloids is intimately linked with the presence of chamber deposits. The family to which *Endoceras* belongs includes some of the largest Palaeozoic invertebrates, with shells of the genus *Cameroceras* attaining a length of approximately 10 m.

Gomphoceras

Europe
Middle Silurian
Length 6–12 cm

A nautiloid in which the shell is short and rapidly expanding. The body chamber is large and rounded, diminishing anteriorly towards a restricted aperture which is 'pinched' in the centre. Behind the body chamber, the shell tapers to a rounded end. The earlier chambers are individually short and together they only equal the length of the expanded body whorl. Externally, the shell of *Gomphoceras* is smooth and without ornament. Very little is known of the internal structures of this genus and as yet it has not been assigned to a definite family, although it is referred to the order Oncocerida. The members of this order have short shells with a ventral siphuncle and siphuncular deposits in aged specimens. Like many of the oncocerids, *Gomphoceras* was probably a seabed scavenger.

Cimomia (Nautiloid)

Worldwide
Upper Jurassic – Oligocene
Diameter across umbilicus parallel to
    aperture 6–10 cm

The fossil record of the living *Nautilus* extends from the Oligocene to the present day and, therefore, the many specimens referred to the genus from Mesozoic and Cainozoic rocks belong to a different genus. Such was the case for individuals previously referred to *Nautilus imperialis* of the Eocene, and they are now associated with the genus *Cimomia*. Like *Nautilus*, this extinct nautiloid has a strongly involute shell of a subglobular to subdiscoidal nature. The outer edge of the whorls is broad and rounded, and is often marked by the flexed line of the suture. A small umbilicus is characteristic of *Cimomia*, as is a pronounced shoulder between the lower part of the side wall of the outer whorl and the umbilicus.

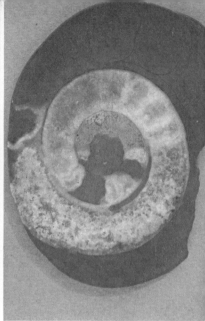

Ammonoidia

Gastrioceras

Worldwide
Upper Carboniferous
Diameter across umbilicus parallel to
aperture 2–5 cm

Like *Reticuloceras*, *Gastrioceras* is a Palaeozoic ammonoid of the suborder Goniatitina. The shell is subdiscoidal to globular in shape, with a moderately large umbilicus. In some species the whorls have ribbed margins, while the ribs do not extend across the surface of the venter. Other species have an ornament of small rather blunt swellings. The suture line of *Gastrioceras* is diagnostic; the prongs of the ventral lobe being rather narrow. The family of goniatites to which *Gastrioceras* is a member, is characterized by a suture with eight lobes. *Gastrioceras* is of considerable stratigraphic importance, with the species *G. listeri* and *G. cumbriense* being used in the zonation of the Namurian of Northwest Europe.

Clymenia

Europe and possibly Western
    Australia and North Africa
Upper Devonian
Diameter across umbilicus parallel to
    aperture 5–8 cm

Ammonoids belonging to the family Clymeniidae are important zone fossils in the Upper Devonian of Europe; *C. laevigata* being of particular value in Germany. *Clymenia* has a discoidal shell in which the outer whorls slightly overhang those inside. The whorls have a characteristic section, with rounded side walls and a rounded to pointed or roof-shaped venter. Several whorls are present and the umbilicus is wide and shallow. The suture lines are relatively simple with a broad rounded lateral lobe and a narrow inner one. *Clymenia* lacks the strong ribs of *Platyclymenia* and the external ornament consists of faint rectilinear growth lines. The clymeniids are primitive ammonoids which are probably derived from goniatite stock.

Ceratites

Europe
Ladinian Stage, Middle Triassic
Diameter across umbilicus parallel to
    aperture 5–9 cm

The genus *Ceratites* has a discoidal shell with a wide shallow umbilicus. Each whorl partly embraces the preceding one and increases in height towards the aperture. In cross-section, the whorls are rather box-like with a broad venter. The ornament of *Ceratites* is coarse, consisting of strong ribs which bear tubercules or nodular projections near the umbilical and outer margins. The ribs are interrupted over the venter. *Ceratites* is characterized by the presence of a ceratitic suture, in which the saddles are rounded and the lobes subdivided or denticulate. *C. nodosus* is a well-known species from Germany which is typically robust with strong ribs and a smooth venter. The specific name is particularly apt and is based on the presence of large nodes.

Echioceras

Worldwide
Lower Jurassic
Diameter across umbilicus parallel to
    aperture 3–6 cm

Echioceras is a small- to medium-sized ammonite, the shell of which is many whorled and evolute in character. The umbilicus is very wide; a slight depression occurring around the inner whorls of the shell. A distinct single keel marks the peripheral wall of each whorl (venter), while pronounced widely spaced ribs ornament the sides. The ribs are finer on the inner whorls but become stronger, straighter, and more widely spaced on the outer ones. There is also a tendency for these ribs to fade towards the keel of the outer whorls. The species *E. raricostatum* is important in subdivision of the Lower Jurassic of Northwest Europe since it marks the uppermost level of the Sinemurian beds.

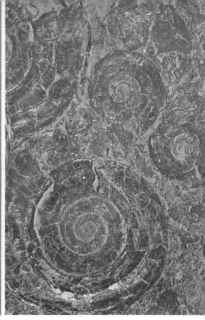

Liparoceras

Europe, North Africa, Indonesia
Lower Jurassic
Diameter across umbilicus parallel to
     aperture 8–12 cm

Individuals referred to the genus *Liparoceras* have a limited geological range within the upper part of the Lower Jurassic. Their shells are of medium size with the outer whorls showing a rapid increase in height and width. This tends to give the involute shell a rather globular appearance. The umbilicus is effectively reduced in size and is deep. The ribbing of *Liparoceras* varies from fine to coarse and is usually continuous across the broad venter. Two rows of swollen tubercules ornament the side walls. In some species a single rib on the side wall divides into two over the venter. The suture line of *Liparoceras* is frequently visible on well-preserved specimens and is characterized by a prominent outer saddle and large first lobe.

Psiloceras

Worldwide
Lower Jurassic
Diameter across umbilicus parallel to
     aperture 3–6 cm

Like many other ammonites figured in this guide, *Psiloceras* is important in the subdivision of the Jurassic period into stages and zones. It is a small ammonite, the shell of which is moderately evolute and compressed. The umbilicus is described as wide or open, while the venter or peripheral wall is bluntly rounded. In some species, blunt sporadic ribs may be present on the lateral walls, but usually the shell is smooth except for fine growth lines. When seen, the suture lines of *Psiloceras* can be described as simple, although the saddles in some species do have a complex leaf-like pattern. In many cases, the delicate shells of *Psiloceras* are found crushed on bedding planes and are often replaced by iron pyrites.

Amaltheus

Europe, North Africa, USSR, North
  America, Canada
Lower Jurassic
Diameter across umbilicus parallel to
  aperture 7–10 cm

The shell of *Amaltheus* is flattened and
discoidal with an acute outer edge.
This type of shell is termed **oxycone**
and although the umbilicus of many
oxycone shells is very narrow, that of
Amaltheus is moderately open. The
outer edge of the shell is keeled and
serrated or corded. In most species, the
external ornament consists of smooth
slightly S-shaped ribs but the shell
surface is furrowed longitudinally or
ornamented with tubercules. The aperture of *Amaltheus* is characterized by
the presence of a long process at the
external margin. Where seen, the suture
line reveals deep lobes and saddles
which are much subdivided. *A. mar-
garitatus* is one of five zone fossils for
the Pliensbachian (Lower Jurassic) of
Northwest Europe.

Dactylioceras

Worldwide
Lower Jurassic
Diameter across umbilicus parallel to
  aperture 4–8 cm

Dactylioceras is one of the best known
of all ammonites, the species *D. com-
mune* being a common specimen in
most palaeontological teaching collections. The shell has many whorls
which hardly overlap each other and
has an appearance somewhat similar to
a coiled snake. In some cases, the
heads of serpents have been carved on
the anterior portion of the specimen
shell to complete the effect! The umbilicus is wide but not very deep.
Strong ribs ornament the shell, some
are simple in character while others
are seen to fork at the periphery. The
ribs are either straight or directed
slightly forwards, towards the aperture.
By comparison with other ammonites,
Dactylioceras is medium sized. The
species *D. tenuicostatum* is used as a
zone fossil for part of the Lower
Jurassic throughout Northwest Europe.

Hildoceras

Europe, Africa, Asia
Lower Jurassic
Diameter across umbilicus parallel to
aperture 4–10 cm

Hildoceras is a rather distinct ammonite in which the shell is somewhat
flattened and the whorls have a rather
square cross-section. The outer whorls
do not overhang the inner ones to any
great extent and the umbilicus is wide.
In some species, lateral depressions
can be traced from the aperture to the
innermost whorls. Strong ribs are
present on the peripheral side of the
depressions, but are absent on the
umbilical side. A strong keel is present;
its character being emphasized by the
occurrence of broad lateral grooves. In
specimens where it is possible to
see the suture line, the lobes are
wider than the saddles and the suture
edge has an almost serrated appearance. *Hildoceras* is used as a zone fossil
for part of the Lower Jurassic.

Stephanoceras

Worldwide
Lower Middle Jurassic
Diameter across umbilicus parallel to
aperture 8–16 cm

Stephanoceras is a moderately evolute
ammonoid in which the whorls are
stout with a rounded exterior margin.
In cross-section the whorls are almost
circular with little overlap. The umbilicus is relatively deep and wide, and
the ribbing of the inner whorls is more
closely packed than that of the outer
ones. Strong ribs are one of the
characteristic features of *Stephanoceras*. These are straight but branch
towards the centre of the side wall,
with two or three subsidiary ribs
crossing the venter. Pronounced nodes
or tubercules may occur at the point
where the ribs divide. The suture line
is strongly folded and divided into
small auxiliary lobes. *S. humphriesi-
anum* is one of the zone fossils of the
Bajocian (Middle Jurassic) of Northwest Europe.

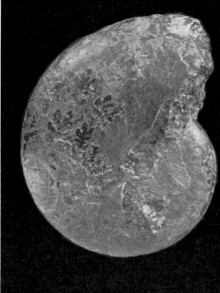

Perisphinctes

Worldwide
Upper Jurassic
Diameter across umbilicus parallel to
    aperture 10–30 cm

Perisphinctes is a large to gigantic form in which the outer whorls hardly overhang the inner ones and have a rounded cross-section; the whole shell having the coiled serpent-like appearance of *Dactylioceras*. Sharply defined closely packed ribs ornament the inner whorls of *Perisphinctes*, while the outer whorls are marked by widely spaced coarse wedge-shaped ridges. The aperture of *Perisphinctes* is simple without constriction. In many-whorled shells such as this, the centres of buoyancy and gravity are very close together and the animal was probably capable of rapid positional changes within its environment. Like *Dactylioceras tenuicostatum*, the species *P. plicatilis* and *P. cautisnigrae* are used in the zonation of part of this period in Northwest Europe.

Phylloceras

Worldwide
Jurassic – Lower Cretaceous
Diameter across umbilicus parallel to
    aperture 4–10 cm

The shell of *Phylloceras* is of medium size, with the outer whorl considerably overlapping the inner ones resulting in a small umbilicus marked by a gentle slope. The shell surface is ornamented by numerous fine raised lines; no strong ribs disrupt the rather smooth nature of the shell. In specimens where the thin outer shell is missing, it is possible to note that the suture line of *Phylloceras* is very complex; the forward directed saddles have much divided leaf-shaped endings. This complex suture line is thought to characterize ammonites that lived a free-swimming life in the open seas and its elaboration would also suggest that *Phylloceras* spent some of its life in deep water.

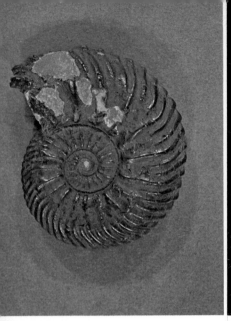

Cardioceras

Europe, North America, Asia
Upper Jurassic
Diameter across umbilicus parallel to
   aperture 4–8 cm

Cardioceras is a small- to medium-sized ammonite, in which the outer whorls partially cover the subsequent inner ones. The umbilical area is rather narrow but deep, exhibiting the tight coiling of the innermost whorls. Each whorl has a somewhat triangular cross-section, a strong central keel being present on the periphery. Strong ribs pass outwards from the umbilical margin of each whorl to cross over both the lateral shell surface and the keel and are even stronger on the inner whorls. The presence of the ribs over the peripheral area gives the keel a rather serrated appearance. A characteristic pattern of ribbing exists where shorter outer ribs occur between the main ribs noted above. The latter are also seen to fork towards the outer margins of the test. *Cardioceras* is used as a zone fossil for part of this period in Northwest Europe.

Hamites

Northern Hemisphere
Lower Cretaceous
Diameter across umbilicus parallel to
   aperture 8–14 cm

Hamites is an example of an heteromorph ammonite, the shell of which is coiled in an open plane spiral so that the chambers occur along three separated subparallel shafts. To achieve this, the shell undergoes two major turns in the growth direction. The diameter of the circular to slightly compressed shell increases gradually along its length. In some forms the ribs are quite closely packed but in others they tend to be separated or distant. The prominence of the ribs is also a variable feature with both fine and coarse types being common. In all cases the ribs are continuous over the venter. Some species of *Hamites* may be almost smooth but none are noted for the presence of nodular tubercles.

Hoplites

Europe, Mexico, Middle East
Upper part of Lower Cretaceous
Diameter across umbilicus parallel to
 aperture 4–8 cm

The shell of *Hoplites* is rather involute and of medium size. In section the whorls have a rather rectangular appearance, the whole shell being somewhat depressed or flattened. The lateral walls of the shell are ornamented with prominent ribs which arise from a tubercle or high spot bordering the umbilicus and extend upwards to the venter. The ribs are branched or zigzag in character; they do not extend over the venter. In some forms of *Hoplites* the rib endings occur opposite each other, but in others they alternate. This difference is of evolutionary significance and is of stratigraphic value to the palaeontologist. *H. dentatus* is the zone fossil for Lower Middle Albian (Lower Cretaceous) of Northwest Europe.

Pachydiscus

Worldwide
Upper Cretaceous
Diameter across umbilicus parallel to
 aperture 6–10 cm

Pachydiscus has a rather compressed shell in which the whorls overlap to a limited extent. The whorls are high with an oval- to flat-sided section. Ribs are present but, instead of extending over the total height of the side wall, they are divided into short umbical and ventrolateral sections. The latter are interrupted on the venter, which is smooth in most species. In one or two varieties the ribs may be of little importance and the shell almost smooth. The umbilicus of *Pachydiscus* is rather wide and of moderate depth. This genus is of importance in the Campanian and Maastrichtian stages of the Upper Cretaceous, where *P. neubergicus* represents the last but one ammonite zone of the Cretaceous period.

Hibolites

Worldwide
Jurassic – Lower Cretaceous
Length 4–8 cm

Actinocamax

Worldwide
Middle and Upper Cretaceous
Length 6–8 cm

Hibolites is a representative of an extinct group of molluscs called the belemnites. These are the only common fossils of a class (Dibranchiata) that is now represented by the squid, cuttle fish, and octopus. The belemnites resemble a squid in the form of their soft parts but their skeletons are quite different from other dibranchiate forms and consist of a **guard, phragmacone**, and **pro-ostracum**. The guard is solid and robust and is the part of the skeleton usually found as a fossil. The phragmacone has the form of a chambered cone, the front of which is greatly extended to form the pro-ostracum. In *Hibolites* the guard is elongate with a bulbous posterior region. The taper towards the anterior end is pronounced and gives the guard a bomb-shaped appearance.

Like *Hibolites*, *Actinocamax* is a dibranchiate mollusc of the order Belemnoidea. It has a cylindrical to broadly funnel-shaped guard with a short but very deep ventral furrow. The guard is round in cross-section and constructed by the successive deposition of sheaths of calcareous fibres. In many specimens this structure is revealed by the 'peeling away' or foliation of the layers. The phragmacone of *Actinocamax* is not deeply inserted into the guard and therefore the conical depression to the front of the guard is shallow. In *Actinocamax*, the surface of the guard is smooth while the posterior end is characterized by the presence of a small pointed extension. Like other elongate cylindrical fossils, the guards of *Actinocamax* may provide evidence for palaeocurrent directions.

Echinodermata

The echinoderms possess skeletons formed by the deposition of calcite crystals. Most fossil groups have living representatives but the blastoids and cystoids, for example, are extinct. Of the various groups, the echinoids possess a somewhat box-like skeleton which has five distinct radiating **ambulacral areas** (composed of two rows of pored plates) alternating with five **interambulacral areas**. Echinoids may be either **regular** or **irregular** varieties; the classification depending on the position of the mouth and anus and the tendency towards bilateral symmetry in the irregular forms.

In the crinoids or sea-lilies, a five-fold symmetry is characteristic and the skeleton is divided into a **crown** and **pelma**.

The starfish (Asteroidea) have five arms of variable length and thickness, and unlike those of the brittlestars (Ophiuroidea) merge gradually with the area of the central disc. Large numbers of ossicles cover the arms, floor, the ambulacral grooves and form a frame for the mouth.

Crinozoa

Eucalyptocrinites

Europe, North America
Silurian — Devonian
Calyx width 2·5—4 cm

Eucalyptocrinites is a member of the crinozoan echinoderms. It is characterized by the fusion of the cup plates to form a rigid structure. Above the basal plates, the cup is perfectly pentamerous. The position and relationship of the arms is also diagnostic with all twenty resting in recesses within the tegmen. This gives the upper part of the skeleton a compact rather elongate appearance. The anus is raised slightly above the level of the arms to prevent waste material fouling the feeding mechanism of the animal. The stem of *Eucalyptocrinites* has a distinctive appearance with two types of columnals being present. At the distal end of the stem, numerous branches occur which act as an anchor.

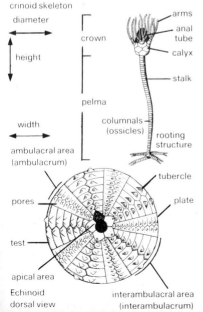

crinoid skeleton

diameter

crown

height

arms

anal tube

calyx

stalk

pelma

width

columnals (ossicles)

rooting structure

ambulacral area (ambulacrum)

tubercle

pores

plate

test

apical area

Echinoid dorsal view

interambulacral area (interambulacrum)

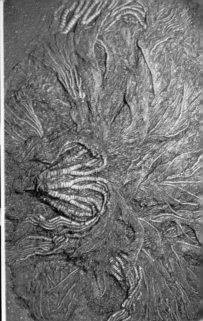

Amphoracrinus

North America, Europe
Lower Carboniferous
Calyx width 2·5–4 cm

Amphoracrinus has a low ovoid to somewhat spherical cup or calyx. There are three **basal** plates on the calyx, followed by a second row of six plates, consisting of five large radials and one smaller interradial. The radials are usually higher than they are wide. Two rows of fused arm plates (**brachials**) occur above the radials, but in this area the number of plates is increased by the appearance of numerous interradial plates. An important feature of the upper surface of *Amphoracrinus* is the **tegmen**, a cover of small hexagonal plates which are extended to form a tube at the end of which is the anus. Ten to thirty arm branches may occur, and unlike those of *Pentacrinites*, they are biserial. The stem of *Amphoracrinus* is rounded in cross-section.

Pentacrinites (Pentacrinus)

Europe, North America
Triassic – Recent
Calyx width 2·5–5 cm

Although complete skeletons of the sea-lily *Pentacrinites* can reach over 1 m in height, the calyx is comparatively small. It is also cup- or bowl-shaped with three rows of plates. The radials are large and overhang the stem, while the basals and **infrabasals** are very small. The presence of infrabasal plates between the basals and stem denotes the **dicyclic** condition in *Pentacrinites* and other crinoids. The arms are very long with many branches and small pinnules. *Pentacrinites* also has a long rather slender stem which bears numerous hair-like **cirri**. These arise in distinct whorls from ossicles which have a very diagnostic star-shaped cross-section. The ossicle surface is also characterized by the presence of five raised petal-like areas. *Pentacrinites* fossils are particularly well known from Lias (Lower Jurassic) sediments.

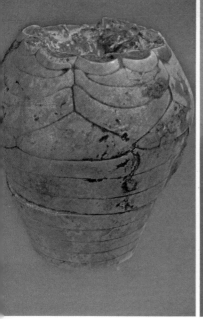

Apiocrinites (Apiocrinus)

Europe
Jurassic
Diameter 3–4 cm

The calyx of *Apiocrinites* is large, with the fusion between the upper ossicles of the stem and the basal plates of the cup giving a very streamlined form. In well-preserved specimens, it is possible to separate the calyx from the stem at the junction between the five large **basal** plates and the uppermost and largest stem ossicle. Above the basal plates, there are five smaller **radials** which are often indented on their upper surface. Four rows of **brachials** then occur above the radials; which are fixed into the upper part of the cup. The first two rows have five plates, the second two have ten smaller ones, with ten arms arising from these plates. The stem of *Apiocrinites* is long and cylindrical with an expanded holdfast at the lower end.

Marsupites

Europe, North America
Upper Cretaceous
Width across calyx 3–5 cm

Marsupites is a large-plated crinoid which lacks the stem so characteristic of other genera. The cup is perfectly pentamerous in character having three rows of five plates. At the base of the cup the position normally reserved for the attachment of the stem is occupied by a large plate. All of the plates have a pattern of well-defined ridges, that sometimes appear to radiate outwards from a raised central point on the plate. The upper plates of the cup have small crescentic facets indicating the position of the arms. When found, complete specimens reveal that the arms are comparatively short and rather small with a number of slender subdivisions called **pinnules**. *Marsupites* was adapted for life in the open sea.

Pentremites

North and South America
Carboniferous
Height 3–5 cm

The blastoid echinoderms are characterized by a pronounced radial symmetry, a uniform arrangement of calyx plates, and compact bud-like thecal cups. *Pentremites* is the classic example of this with the five ambulacral rays projecting outwards from the mouth. The mouth and five small outlets (**spiracles**) for the water circulatory system occur on the upper surface. The ambulacral rays form V-shaped depressions or grooves and are easily identified by the presence of numerous small cover plates. Small deltoid and larger radial plates occur between the rays with the base having three outwardly directed basals. Like the crinoids, the blastoids were fixed echinoderms. They reached their peak during the Carboniferous; *Pentremites, and Cordyloblastus* from Europe being well-known examples.

Macrocystella

Europe
Lower Ordovician
Height 2·5–4 cm

Macrocystella is a stalked echinoderm known only from the Lower Ordovician of England and Germany. Like other echinoderms, it is made up of a variety of calcareous plates, with the skeleton comprising a sac-shaped body or **theca** regularly arranged; each plate has an ornament of radial ridges. Five arms arise from the uppermost plates of the theca; the arms dividing into two after only a short distance. The arms and stem are made up of numerous rounded ossicles (plates) which in both cases tend to become smaller away from the theca. *Macrocystella* and its relatives were primitive attached inhabitants of ancient sea-floor environments.

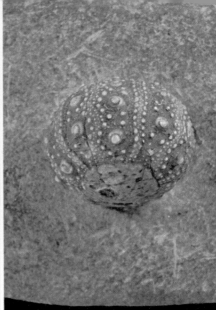

Echinoidea

Archaeocidaris

Europe, North America, India
Carboniferous — Permian
Diameter 3—6 cm

Archaeocidaris is one of the first known representatives of the echinoid family. In life, it had a flexible test in which the plates tended to overlap each other. The interambulacral areas have four rows of plates, which is regarded as a primitive condition in the evolution of the cidaroids. In general terms, the test is subspherical with a slight flattening apparent on both upper and lower surfaces. The interambulacral plates have large tubercules and on occasion numerous elongate spines are found in association with the specimen. The mouth and arms of *Archaeocidaris* occur centrally on the ventral and dorsal surfaces and the specimen is referred to as being a regular echinoid. It is probable that it lived in shallow-water environments.

Acrosalenia

Europe, North Africa
Upper Triassic — Lower Cretaceous
Diameter 2—4 cm

A small regular echinoid in which the test is rounded in outline and flattened dorsoventrally. Large tubercules ornament the plates of the interambulacra, two rows revealing the number of plate rows in each area. The apical system is large and central, but the anus has moved slightly off centre. The ambulacra are distinct and narrow and marked by paired rows of small tubercules. On the ventral surface the mouth is seen as central and very large. Sometimes the long robust spines that articulated with the large interambulacral tubercules are found in association with the test. The first doubtful recordings of *Acrosalenia* are from Triassic rocks, but the major discoveries are from Upper Jurassic to Lower Cretaceous sediments.

Plesiechinus
Europe, North America
Jurassic
Diameter 4—6 cm

Plesiechinus is a medium-sized regular echinoid with a flattened, subrounded test. The dorsal surface is smooth with the straight ambulacra radiating from the raised apical system. A large oval aperture marks the site of the anus and is found in the posterior interambulacral area. On the underside the mouth is central, large, and flower-like in appearance. Also small tubercules ornament the various plates which could have only supported short weak spines. By comparison with the similarly structured living echinoid, *Apatopygus*, it is thought that *Plesiechinus* rested on the sea-floor and fed on detrital material. It probably existed in shallow-water environments.

Clypeus
Europe, North Africa
Middle — Upper Jurassic
Diameter 5—10 cm

Clypeus is an irregular echinoid of medium to large size. It has a low flattened profile and is circular in outline. On the ventral surface the mouth is almost central, the five sub-parallel interambulacral areas radiating to the edge of the test. The ventral surface is slightly indented towards the mouth. On the upper surface the apical system of plates is slightly off centre. The well-developed petaloid dorsal interambulacral areas narrow towards the edge of the test and the apical system. The anus of *Clypeus* occurs outside the apical system, a longitudinal groove marking its presence. During life, *Clypeus* existed partially buried in the sediment on the sea-floor. Numerous species are to be found in the Middle Jurassic rocks of Europe.

Nucleolites

Europe, Africa
Middle Jurassic — Upper Cretaceous
Midline length 2—4 cm

Like *Clypeus*, a close relative, *Nucleolites* has a limited palaeogeographical distribution. It appears at the same time in the geological record, but survives almost until the end of the Mesozoic era. *Nucleolites* is small to medium sized with a subcircular outline, the widest area of the test occurring behind the centre. On the ventral surface the mouth has migrated slightly towards the front of the test and the five ambulacral areas are straight and rather narrow. Dorsally, the ambulacra are more petaloid but still straighter than those of *Clypeus*. The anus of *Nucleolites* is to be found in a deep notch which passes inwards from the rear edge of the test.

Conulus

Europe, North Africa, Asia, North
  America
Upper Cretaceous
Height 3—4 cm

Conulus, like *Echinocorys*, has a flat ventral surface, with the main body of the test having a hemispherical or highly conical form. The mouth and anus occur on the ventral surface; the former occupies the central position while the latter is sited on the back margin. The ambulacra are rather narrow and straight and are clearly visible on both surfaces. Numerous small tubercules ornament the interambulacral areas. Unlike related forms, *Conulus* has no internal support structures that strengthen the test. The overall shape of *Conulus* makes it a distinctive fossil which is abundant in the Chalk of Europe, but very little is known about the mode of life of this animal.

Echinocorys

Europe, Asia, North America
Upper Cretaceous – Palaeocene
Midline length 5–8 cm

Echinocorys is a rather large irregular echinoid with a subconical test and a smooth surface texture. The base or ventral surface is flattened with a cresentic depression which contains the mouth and anus. The mouth is positioned close to the anterior border while the anus, which extends downwards beyond the general level of the surface, occurs near the back edge. The ambulacra of *Echinocorys* are not as distinct as those of other echinoids and are not petaloid in outline. No large tubercules occur on the test plates but these neat rows of interlocking plates are one of the attractive features of this well-known fossil.

Micraster

Europe, Cuba, Mediterranean,
  Madagascar
Upper Cretaceous – Palaeocene
Midline length 5–7 cm

Although *Micraster* is frequently thought of in terms of being a zone fossil for the Upper Cretaceous of Europe, the genus in fact had a fairly wide geographic distribution during the Upper Cretaceous and Palaeocene. *Micraster* is a heart-shaped urchin characterized by a flattened lower surface on which the mouth is sited anteriorly. The test has an inflated appearance, the upper surface being indented by five petaloid arms (ambulacra) which radiate from the centre. The anterior ambulacrum runs into a deep groove which forms the notch of the heart shape. The anus of *Micraster* is sited posteriorly, behind and below a dorsal ridge. *M. cortestudinaris* is the species used as a zone fossil for the Upper Cretaceous.

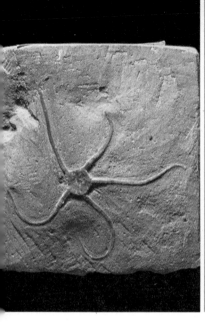

Asterozoa

Ophioderma

Worldwide
Lower Jurassic — Recent
Central disc diameter 1·5—3 cm

Although some texts claim that *Ophioderma* is a genus limited to the present day, others record species such as *O. egertoni* from sediments of the Lower Jurassic. *Ophioderma* is a typical brittle-star echinoderm with long thin arms and a distinct central disc. The arms are inserted laterally and are firmly incorporated into the body of the disc. They are also rounded, tapering away from the disc to a fine terminal point. The disc itself has a well-defined five-fold symmetry with the mouth being placed on the ventral surface. During feeding, food is passed along the ambulacral grooves of the arms into the petaloid mouth. The first brittle-stars appeared in the Lower Ordovician; they are essentially shallow burrowers and surface crawlers.

Calliderma

Europe
Upper Cretaceous — Oligocene and
  Recent
Individual size 12—25 cm

This is a well-known representative of the starfish group of echinoderms. It is moderately large with a broad central disc and short arms. The arms, unlike those of a brittle-star, are relatively indistinct, fusing evenly with the body or disc area. On the outer edges of the skeleton the marginal plates are large and clearly defined. On the disc, however, the upper and lower surfaces are covered with a pavement of small close-fitting plates. The skeleton is flattened with a star-shaped outline. As with the brittle-stars the mouth is present on the lower ventral surface and linked to the arms by means of the ambulacral grooves. *C. smithiae* is a common species from the Cenomanian stage of the Upper Cretaceous.

Arthropoda

The various arthropod groups are distinguished by the possession of a segmented body and hardened external skeleton. Crustaceans, myriapods, and insects are living examples with good fossil records, but the most important group from the palaeontological view is the Trilobita. These are characterized by a three-fold division of the body in both transverse and longitudinal directions. Transversely, the body is divided into the head (**cephalon**), a middle region (**thorax**), and a tail (**pygidium**). Along its length the body is divided into a central axial region and two lateral areas. Individual segments can often be distinguished in the head, thorax, and tail. The axial region of the head is called the **glabella**, while the lateral regions bear the eyes and are usually subdivided into **free** and **fixed cheek** areas. The posterior corners of the headshield are termed the **genal angles**, although in some forms they are extended to form **genal spines**.

Trilobita

Olenus

Northern Europe, North America, Asia
Upper Cambrian
Midline length 2–4 cm

A rather small-sized trilobite where the head is larger than the tail and has a narrow raised border and short genal spines. The central glabella area of the headshield is rounded anteriorly and marked by three pairs of grooves. Short ridges connect the glabella with the small but distinct eyes. The facial suture of *Olenus* cuts the rear margin of the headshield inside the genal angle. Behind the head there are thirteen to fifteen thoracic segments, which have a rather spiny appearance, and a small triangular tail. *Olenus* is particularly well known from northern Europe; together with *Olenellus* and *Paradoxides* it is used to subdivide the Cambrian into Lower, Middle, and Upper Stages.

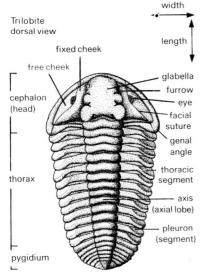

Trilobite dorsal view

fixed cheek
free cheek
cephalon (head)
thorax
pygidium

width
length
glabella
furrow
eye
facial suture
genal angle
thoracic segment
axis (axial lobe)
pleuron (segment)

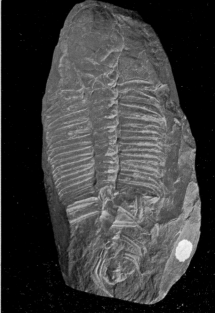

Agnostus

Europe, Asia
Cambrian – Ordovician
Adult size 10–25 mm

Agnostus is representative of a diminutive family of trilobites that lived during the .Cambrian and Ordovician periods and is found in the Upper Cambrian of Europe and China. The head or tail regions of *Agnostus* are of equal size and the thorax consists of only two segments. The animal is without eyes or facial sutures on the headshield, and the head is recognized by the presence of a longitudinal furrow in front of the glabella. The tail is divided into two or three lobes and two small spines break the rounded outline of the border. Adult specimens grew to a maximum of 10–15 mm, a specimen measuring 25 mm being looked upon as a giant.

Paradoxides

Europe, North America, Africa,
  Australia
Middle Cambrian
Midline length 6–16 cm

A rather spectacular trilobite with some individuals reaching 45 cm in length. The head is much larger than the minute tail and the genal spines are equal to half the length of the body. Both thorax and tail have a spiny appearance; the thorax having between sixteen to twenty-one segments. The spines of the thorax and tail show a gradual increase in size posteriorly, although the second thoracic segment is characteristically longer than either one or three. *Paradoxides* with the characters noted above, coupled with an extended glabella and large eyes, is an easily identifiable fossil. It has a limited time range and is used in the division of the Cambrian period.

Kjerulfia

Northern Europe
Lower Cambrian
Midline length 5–8 cm

A medium- to large-sized trilobite where the headshield is subtriangular in outline with short genal spines and dwarfs the minute tail. *Kjerulfia* has a lobed glabella with the first lobe expanded sideways; the large eyes are linked to the glabella by short ridges. Sixteen or seventeen segments make up the thorax, each segment bearing a short axial spine. Like its relatives *Nevadia*, *Callavia*, and *Olenellus*, *Kjerulfia* is important in the study of the geography of the Cambrian period. It is probable that *Kjerulfia* dug burrows in the soft sediment of the seafloor. The tracks, trails, and burrows of trilobites such as *Kjerulfia* are of increasing importance in the study of Lower Palaeozoic environments.

Ampyx

Europe, North America
Lower – Middle Ordovician
Midline length 3–5 cm

Ampyx is a rather small but interesting trilobite. In general terms the head, thorax, and tail are of approximately equal lengths, but the presence of long glabellar and genal spines gives the headshield increased dimensions. The glabellar spine is the forward extension of the inflated glabella. *Ampyx* has no eyes and the facial suture cuts the posterior margin of the headshield. Six segments make up the thorax each having a deep-furrow on either side of the axis. The tail also has a prominent axis but little or no evidence of segments occurs outside the axial area. The spines of *A. tetragonus gigas* are extremely long and explanation of their function still eludes the palaeontologist.

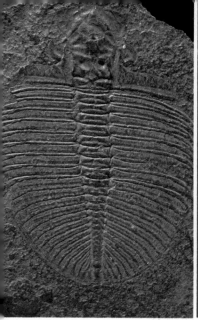

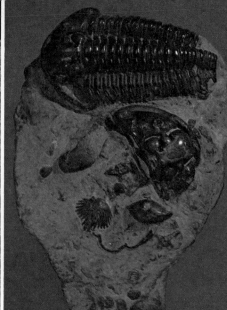

Ogygiocaris

Northern Europe, Argentine
Lower — Middle Ordovician
Midline length 5—8 cm

Ogygiocaris lived over 450 million years ago. The head and tail are of roughly equal size, with the rather small genal spines reaching back as far as the third body segment. The glabella is well defined with faint furrows present level with the eyes. Distinct facial sutures occur on the headshield, the suture lines running from in front of the glabella, around the inside margin of the eye, and back to cut the rear border of the headshield inside the genal angle. The thorax has eight segments each of which is marked by a distinct furrow. *Ogygiocaris* has a rounded tail, the axis of which tapers backwards. The tail segments are fused and a wide border is characteristic of the genus.

Calymene

Worldwide
Silurian — Devonian
Midline length 3—6 cm

Calymene is a medium-sized trilobite, the head of which is larger than the tail. The glabella has a distinctive appearance standing high above the rest of the headshield and possessing three prominent lobes on each side. The pair of lobes furthest from the glabella are larger than the other two. *Calymene* has no genal spines and the facial suture is seen to cut the rounded genal angle. Thirteen segments make up the thorax, each being marked by a deep furrow on either side of the axis. However, the tail is quite small with only six segments. *C. blumenbachii* is one of the better-known species of the genus; its profile forms part of the coat of arms of the town of Dudley, England.

Onnia

Europe, North Africa, South America
Ordovician
Midline length 4–6 cm

Onnia is a member of a very distinct group of trilobites known as the trinucleids and is found in sediments of Middle and Upper Ordovician age. The head of *Onnia* is much larger than the tail and the long genal spines extend well beyond the posterior tail margin. No eyes or facial sutures are visible on the headshield. A large expanded glabella and distinct pitted margin are characteristic. Four rows of pits occur on the margin, the outer row having a greater number of smaller pits than those inside. The thorax has only six segments and the tail is rather flat on either side of the axis.

Phacops

Worldwide
Silurian – Devonian
Midline length 2·5–5 cm

This genus is characterized by the compact nature of its skeleton. The headshield is dominated by the large glabella which widens forwards. *Phacops* has large eyes and it is often possible to recognize individual lenses. There are no genal spines, and the edges of the body segments and the tail are rounded which enabled the animal to roll itself into a tight ball; enrolment was common to most trilobites and served to protect the soft underside of the animal. As in *Dalmanites*, the facial suture of *Phacops* cuts the border of the head in front of the genal angle. Examples of *Phacops* have been discovered in many European localities.

Bumastus

Worldwide
Middle Ordovician — Lower Silurian
Midline length 6–10 cm

An elongate trilobite in which the head and tail are of equal size. The axial region of the headshield is poorly developed while that of the thorax is smooth and very broad. On the headshield, the eyes are well developed and bordered on the inside by the short facial suture. The latter runs from the outer edge of the head, around the eye, and to the back edge of the head. Between eight to ten segments can be counted along the length of the thorax, and no grooves disrupt the smooth nature of the thoracic region. The rounded tail lacks any segmentation or furrowing. *Bumastus* is very similar to both *Illaenus* and *Isotelus* and care must be taken in identification.

Dalmanites

Worldwide
Silurian — Devonian
Midline length 4–7 cm

A well-known form, *Dalmanites*, is 'streamlined' with long genal spines directed backwards along the borders of the thorax. The tail is slightly smaller than the head; a long tail spine characterizing some species. The head is spade-shaped or crescent-like with the glabella widening anteriorly. A well-defined facial suture divides the head, the rear line of the suture cutting the headshield in front of the genal angle. The eyes of *Dalmanites* are large and crescentic in outline. Eleven segments can be counted in the thorax and seven in the pygidium. *D. myops* is a well-known species from the Wenlock series.

Encrinurus

Worldwide
Middle Ordovician — Silurian
Midline length 4–6 cm

Encrinurus is a small- to medium-sized trilobite characterized in part by an ornament of large tubercles. The head is larger than the tail and the glabella is seen to expand forward beyond the border of the headshield. The eyes occur on short stalks to the side of the glabella. The facial sutures run parallel to the margin and cut the outside border of the headshield above the genal angle. Eleven or twelve segments are present in the thorax each of which is clearly recognizable. The tail of *Encrinurus* is subtriangular in outline but it is clearly longer than it is broad, ornamented by three lines of tubercules. *E. punctatus* and *E. variolaris* are well-known species from the Wenlock series (Middle Silurian).

Griffithides

Europe, North America
Carboniferous
Midline length 3–5 cm

Griffithides is a relatively small trilobite with the head and tail of approximately equal size. The head is semi-oval in shape, having small eyes and a glabella that widens towards the frontal margin. It has rounded genal angles and the facial suture cuts the rear border inside the genal angle. The thorax is made up of nine segments with the central area, the axis, having a high strong profile. The tail consists of a number of fused segments with the axis again being strongly developed. Numerous small swellings (tubercles) give *Griffithides* and its Lower Carboniferous relatives a characteristic ornament. Other relatives are among the last trilobites known on Earth. *Griffithides* differs from *Phillipsia*, another Carboniferous opisthoparian, in that it has an inflated glabella and lacks short genal spines.

Other Arthropoda

Arcoscalpellum

Worldwide
Upper Cretaceous – Recent
Height 2–3 cm

Arcoscalpellum is a barnacle, therefore marine, and leads a fixed mode of life. The barnacles are highly specialized crustaceans which secrete an external calcareous shell consisting of fifteen plates. In some cases these may be found as separate entities but usually they are found in association. The body is termed the **capitulum**, and covering plates include a single elongate plate, the **carina**, and four larger body plates, two **terga** and two **scuta**. The plates form a protective shield around the soft parts, with the animal emerging through an operculum. *A. quadratum* from the Eocene is, as its name suggests, very angular in appearance. The plates are marked with horizontal striations which are displaced by the ridges formed within each plate.

Notopocorystes

Europe, Middle and Far East, North
   America
Cretaceous
Carapace length 3–4 cm

Notopocorystes has an ovoid to shield-shaped carapace which is often longer than it is broad. The front of the carapace is rather narrow, and the greatest width is attained slightly above the halfway line. There are two distinct fissures that occur above the orbits and two or more pairs of lateral spines also characterize the genus. The surface of the carapace may be finely granulated or smooth in texture with a median ridge of small nodes or tubercules distinguishing several species. Lateral grooves and tubercules also occur as surface ornament. Many crab fossils are found in calcareous nodules and can often be linked with trace fossils. *Notopocorystes* is a member of the family Raninidae, several genera of which are living today in the East Indies and the Indo-Pacific area.

101

Ostracoda

Hoploparia

Worldwide
Cretaceous – Eocene
Length 8–20 cm

As a lobster, *Hoploparia* is a member of the phylum Arthropoda and therefore a distant relative of the trilobites. The crabs, lobsters, crayfish, shrimps, prawns, and barnacles are grouped together as crustaceans and represent a large variety of marine invertebrates. *Hoploparia* is a small lobster with an elongate body which is slightly compressed laterally. The external skeleton is divided into several areas which cover the head, thorax, and abdomen. The rostrum over the head is long and narrow and the carapace over the body is covered with a fine granular ornament. *Hoploparia* has a segmented abdomen, long legs, and large pincers. Fossils of crustaceans such as *H. gammaroides* are often discovered in the centre of calcareous nodules.

Beyrichia

Europe, North America, Australia
Lower Silurian – Middle Devonian
Hinge line length 1–2 mm

Beyrichia is an example of an extremely important class of Crustacea, called the Ostracoda. The ostracodes range from the Ordovician to the present day, their minute shells being found mostly in mudstones, shales, and muddy limestones. The majority of shells in this class range in size from 0·5–5 mm, although some gigantic forms may reach 20 mm in length. An ostracode shell consists of two valves which are usually of unequal size. The valves articulate by means of a hinge line, with hinge teeth in one valve and sockets in the other. In *Beyrichia*, the surface ornament is nodular with large brood pouches helping to distinguish the female from the male animal. The abundance of ostracodes in the fossil record, together with their small size, make them extremely important to economic geologists and stratigraphers.

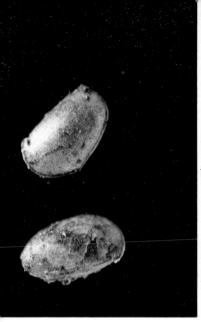

Insecta

Cypridea

Europe, Americas, Africa, Japan
Middle Jurassic — Lower Cretaceous
Length 1–2 mm

Cypridea is an ostracode in which the shell has a rather box-like appearance. Most shells are compressed to moderately convex, with the area near the hinge line (dorsum) almost straight. The valves are of almost equal size with a characteristic beak-like projection on the lower front edge. Where a noticeable difference in size occurs between the valves, it is usually the left valve which is the largest. The surface ornament of *Cypridea* varies with the species. Some are covered with tiny pinprick depressions (**puncta**) while others have a net-like pattern of intersecting crests or ridges. Spines, granules, or tubercles are not common characters of cypridean ornament. Several species of *Cypridea* are common to rocks of Jurassic age throughout Europe.

Insects

Worldwide
Upper Carboniferous — Recent
Variable size

Insects first appeared in the Carboniferous and have become increasingly more numerous, until to date close to a million species have been recorded. The number of types is seemingly endless and they are adapted to live in nearly every ecological niche. Fossil insects, however, are rather poorly known with a pronounced fall off in pre-Cainozoic environments. The best recorded insect faunas occur entombed in **amber** (fossilized resin) or in fine sediments deposited in lakes and lagoons.

The beetles comprise the insect order Coleoptera, and are characterized by the modification of the front wings into horny covers (**elytra**). The elytra and the segments of the abdomen are clearly shown in this specimen collected from the fine ash-rich sediments of Menat in Central France.

Graptolithina

The Graptolithina are colonial marine animals which lived during the Palaeozoic era. They are regarded as relatives of the living pterobranchs and rhabdopleurids and are therefore directly linked with the evolution of the chordates. The graptolites secreted a horny external skeleton made-up of two layers. The first of these was constructed of narrow transverse growth segments and the second and outer one of a layered fibrous tissue. Each colony of graptolites is termed a **rhabdosome**, which comprises a number of branches (**stipes**) which are lined by numerous tube- or cup-like structures (**thecae**). In the rather shrub-like dendroid graptolites there are numerous branches and usually three types of theca, while in the graptoloids the number of branches is restricted (with a trend in reduction from thirty-two to one) and only one type of theca is present. The thread-like extension from the apex of the colony is termed the **nema** which originates from the first cup or **sicula** which also gives rise to the whole colony.

Callograptus
Worldwide
Upper Cambrian — Carboniferous
Branches hair-like
Colony fragments approximately
   4–8 cm

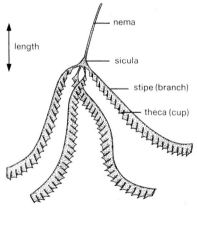

Tetragraptus rhabdosome (colony)

- nema
- length
- sicula
- stipe (branch)
- theca (cup)

Callograptus was an attached form which looked rather like a fern. The rhabdosome shape varied with the species from conical to irregular with the numerous stipes usually branching in pairs. Small strands of connecting tissue (dissepiments) occur intermittently to link the stipes and give the colony strength. *Callograptus* belonged to the same family as *Dictyonema* namely the family Dendrograptidae which lived throughout much of the Palaeozoic era. The dendrograptids are characterized by having three types of thecae. In both *Callograptus* and *Dictyonema* the largest thecae, the autothecae, are directed ventrally. The rather simple structure of *Callograptus* appeared well suited to its mode of life, a fact emphasized by the long range of the genus.

Bryograptus

North West Europe, North America,
Greenland, Australia
Lower Ordovician
Branches hair-like
Colony fragments approximately
4–6 cm

Bryograptus is a member of the dendroid group of graptolites, but unlike Dictyonema it belongs to a family directly linked with the evolution of the graptoloids. Like other members of this family (Anisograptidae), Bryograptus exhibits a reduction in the number of stipes present in the rhabdosome and in the variety of thecal types which are rather simple in structure. The rhabdosome develops from three initial stipes with later branching being of an irregular nature. Bryograptus is found in deposits of Lower Ordovician age in Scandinavia. In Australia the genus is used, along with Clonograptus, as a zone fossil for the lowermost Ordovician sediments.

Tetragraptus

Worldwide
Early Ordovician
Branch length 2–3 cm

The rhabdosome of Tetragraptus consists of four stipes which branch in pairs, the colony having bilateral symmetry. Several species are referred to the genus, the arrangement of the four stipes being diagnostic. In all known species, the thecae are closely packed and occur along one side of the stipe which has a saw-like profile; the thecal cup is simple but sharply pointed in appearance. In some species, the stipes are pendulous while in others they are reclined. Tetragraptids are common in many deposits of Lower Ordovician age, and particularly those of Scandinavia where forms such as T. serra and T. phyllograptoides are found in association with Didymograptus and Phyllograptus.

Phyllograptus
Worldwide
Early Ordovician
Stipe length 2—3 cm

Dichograptus
Worldwide
Lower Ordovician
Stipe length 2—3 cm

As a member of the family *Tetragraptidae*, *Phyllograptus* has a rhabdosome made-up of four branches. These, unlike the more normal forms, are united in the erect (scandent) position and are called **quadriserial**; the colony being cross-shaped in section. The four rows of thecae occur in 'back to back' contact; each theca having a simple slightly curved and elongate form. A considerable overlay occurs between each thecal cup. It is very rare to find specimens of *Phyllograptus* showing all four stipes since most specimens are flattened and show only two stipes in a leaf-like form. The pyritized remains of countless individuals have been found in the black shales of Scandinavia.

Dichograptus has a rhabdosome consisting of eight or less stipes which arise in pairs. The first two pairs are fairly short and of equal length but the third pair is much longer. Large numbers of rather sharply pointed thecae occur along one side of each stipe and are directed outwards at a low angle overlapping each other. A characteristic feature of certain species of *Dichograptus* is a large web-like disc that binds the central region of the rhabdosome. It is possible that this structure played a role in the buoyancy of the colony. Like many other graptolites, *Dichograptus* was thought to have been planktonic in its mode of life.

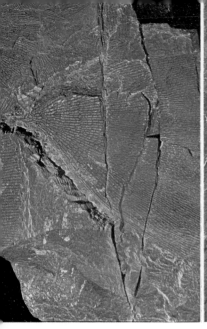

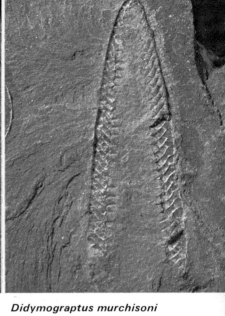

Dictyonema

Worldwide
Upper Cambrian — Lower
 Carboniferous
Branch width 0·1 mm
Colony fragments 3–6 cm

Dictyonema is one of the best known of all graptolites; its conical rhabdosome has been discovered in many countries. The colony of *Dictyonema* although conical in shape varied from nearly cylindrical to almost flat. Numerous stipes make-up the individual colony; these arise in pairs with a degree of regularity. Each straight stipe bears a multitude of thecae which in species such as *D. flabelliforme* are tooth-like in appearance. A nema is present in *Dictyonema* suggesting that the colony may have lived attached to floating 'weed' which would account for the widespread distribution of this genus. It is also probable that *Dictyonema* was rather bell-shaped.

Didymograptus murchisoni

Worldwide
Lower Ordovician
Stipe length 3–6 cm

Graptolites belonging to the genus *Didymograptus* never have more than two stipes. These may hang below the sicula (first thecal cup from which the colony arises) like the prongs of a tuning fork or be raised through various stages to the reclined position. This last occurs where the stipes extend upward and inwards towards the nema. *D. murchisoni* is a well-known pendent form, while *D. extensus* represents the horizontal types. The thecae of *Didymograptus* are usually straight and simple, although they may be slightly curved in some species. European species of *Didymograptus* are well known from South Wales, Brittany, and Scandinavia. Several species of *Didymograptus* are also used in the zonation of the Lower Ordovician of Europe and Australia.

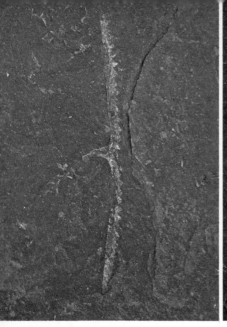

Didymograptus extensus

Worldwide
Lower Ordovician
Width across both branches
   2·5–10 cm

Although the majority of individual specimens referred to the genus *Didymograptus* belong to the tuning fork varieties such as *D. murchisoni* and *D. bifidus*, other species including *D. nicholsoni* and *D. extensus* are characteristic of Ordovician sediments. These species appear to represent different stages in the evolution towards the diplograptid condition; the tuning fork stage is supposedly the most primitive condition and the horizontal or extended type the intermediate one. *D. extensus* has two stipes characterized by the presence of numerous simple straight thecae. In many specimens it is possible to recognize the small triangular sicular between the branches and the thread-like nema at its apex. The didymograptids are very important in the correlation of Lower Ordovician rocks.

Orthograptus

Worldwide
Upper Ordovician – Lower Silurian
Colony length 4–8 cm

Orthograptus is a member of the family Diplograptidae in which the thecae are found on both sides of a single branch. This type of rhabdosome is described as biserial. The thecae of *Orthograptus* are either straight or slightly curved; the two series occurring opposite each other. In some forms, small spines are developed at the mouth of each theca. Large spines are often present at the base of the colony. The wide geographic distribution of *Orthograptus* suggests that like other diplograptids it was planktonic, with the possibility that numerous colonies shared the same float. Several species of *Orthograptus* are found in deposits of Upper Ordovician age in Northwest Europe. They are not, however, used for the purpose of zonation.

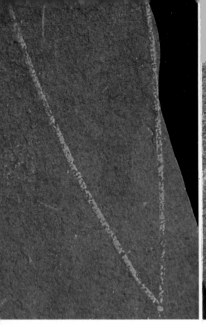

Dicranograptus

Europe, North and South America,
  Australia, Asia
Ordovician
Stipe length 3–5 cm

In form, *Dicranograptus* appears to occupy a position halfway between the two-stiped *Didymograptus* and the single-stiped *Diplograptus*. The rhabdosome is a strange mixture, the lower part having a biserial structure with a row of thecae on each side of the stipe. The colony then branches into two stipes, each of which bears a single row of thecae. The branching stipes form a V-shaped outline. Some dicranograptids have complex S-curved thecae. *Dicranograptus* is thought to represent an important stage in the evolution of the diplograptids. *D. clingani* is used as a zone fossil within the Caradocian series of Britain and other European areas.

Monograptus

Worldwide
Silurian
Varies with species, approximately
  2–15 cm

As the name suggests, the monograptids are a family of single-stiped graptoloids in which the thecae are arranged in a single row. This condition is termed **uniserial**, while the growth of the stipe vertically to enclose the nema is known as **scandent**. As with other generic names, *Monograptus* represents a number of species each of which have individual characteristics. The rhabdosomes may be straight, coiled, or spiral; the thecae pointed, rounded, or elongate. The number of thecae on a monograptid stipe is limited when compared with that of *Dictyonema*; the thecae are also much larger in size. Since Monograptids were common, various species are used in sediment zonation.

Rastrites

Worldwide, except North and South
   America
Lower Silurian
Thecae length 1–3 mm

This graptolite has several characters
which make it unique within the
family Monograptidae. Typically, the
rhabdosome consists of a single stipe
with one row of thecae; but the thin,
thread-like nature of the stipe and the
length of the thecae make *Rastrites*
easily identifiable. The stipe is slightly
curved with a tighter curl in initial
stages of the colony. Each theca is not
only very long but also isolated from
its neighbours, giving the colony a
very 'open' appearance. The mouth of
each thecal unit may be slightly hooked
with small spines present in some
species. The species *R. maximus* is
used as a zone fossil within the
Llandoverian series.

Cyrtograptus

Worldwide, except South America
Middle Silurian
Colonies 5–8 cm

Cyrtograptus is a graptoloid in which a
number of side branches arise from
the main stipe. The latter is generally
spirally coiled and bears thecae of two
distinct forms along its length. At first,
the thecae may be hooked or triangular
in form, whereas later cups become
simple in outline. The branches arising
from the main stipe, do so regularly
and many bear side branches of their
own. *Cyrtograptus* and its relatives are
similar to the monograptids. Apart
from *Cyrtograptus* other graptolites
placed in the family *Cyrtograptidae*
have been discovered in Germany,
Sweden, Poland, and Australia and
several cyrtograptid species are used
in the zonation of the Wenlockian
series of Europe.

Vertebrata

The first animals referred to as vertebrates are the fish-like ostracoderms (shell skinned) of the Silurian and Devonian. These are heavily armoured creatures without jaws and apparently lacking the vertebral column of later groups. Throughout the Late Palaeozoic, Mesozoic, and Cainozoic the vertebrates followed many lines of evolution with successive classes such as the fishes, amphibians, reptiles, and mammals rising to prominence. Complete skeletons of vertebrates are not common but various localities have yielded excellent faunas. The most common remains of vertebrates are the teeth, which withstand the effects of sedimentary processes much better than individual bones. The remains of mammals are rare in pre-Cainozoic faunas, but in the Cainozoic they are extremely useful for the correlation of terrestrial sediments. In the Upper Cretaceous, the dinosaurs of North America are used for similar purposes. These reptiles were the dominant group during the Mesozoic, the amphibians throughout the Carboniferous, and the fish in the Devonian.

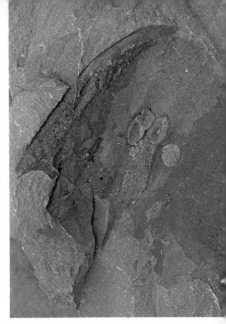

Pisces

Cephalaspis

Europe, Spitzbergen, North America, Asia
Upper Silurian — ? Upper Devonian
Length 38 cm

Cephalaspis is one of the best known of the ostracoderm or 'shell skinned' vertebrates from late Silurian and early Devonian rocks. The whole body is covered with an armour of plates and scales; the upper surface of the skull being covered by a solid bony shield. In Cephalaspis the shield is extended at the rear outside corners to form prominent 'horns' or spines. The eyes occur in the centre of the upper surface, with the 'third eye' represented by the pineal opening placed between them. In front of the eyes there is a small slit for a single nostril and two well-defined lateral sensory organs. The headshield of Cephalaspis is clearly separated from the fish-like trunk. As an agnathan, Cephalaspis has no jaws and the sucker-like mouth is placed on the under surface.

Orodus

Europe, North America
Carboniferous — Permian
Length approximately 5–10 cm

Orodus and other members of the hybodont sharks represent the second stage in the evolution of shark-like fishes — the ancient cladoselachian order. This order arose in the Middle Devonian and was replaced by the more advanced hybodonts during the Carboniferous and Permian periods. The essential differences between the two orders included changes in the fin, jaw, and teeth. In *Orodus*, the teeth are long and wide with a pronounced cusp or crown in an almost central position. The individual teeth occur in rows or series and are replaced when damaged or shed. The cusps of front teeth may be sharper than those at the back of the jaws. Outside the highest cusp, the teeth have a rippled or serrated appearance. The teeth and elongate fin spines of *Orodus* are among the more common vertebrate remains in Carboniferous sediments.

Myliobatis

Europe, North America, Africa, Asia, Australasia
Upper Cretaceous — Recent
Individual tooth-plate width 3–6 cm

Many marine deposits of Upper Cretaceous and Tertiary age, yield excellent tooth plates of the eagle ray, *Myliobatis*. The eagle rays, like the sharks, are cartilaginous fish belonging to the class chondrichthyes. Since cartilage is rarely preserved in fossil records, it is the teeth of *Myliobatis* that usually indicate its presence in fossil marine communities. These are wide and flattened with the individual tooth plates packed together to form large crushing structures. Eagle rays are mostly bottom-dwelling fishes; the robust structure of the teeth indicating that they fed on shell fish. The body of living myliobatids is short with the fins showing a very large lateral expansion.

Ptychodus

Europe, North America, Africa, Asia
Cretaceous
Individual tooth width 2—4 cm

Ptychodus, like *Orodus*, is a hybodont shark, but unlike the latter it is rather specialized, having flattened teeth which were used for crushing shell fish. The ptychodonts arose from the hybodonts during the Cretaceous and occupied their particular niche for some 60 million years. *Ptychodus* teeth are rather square in shape and robust in structure. They are flattened and the centre of the tooth looks like a strongly defined fingerprint, which is surrounded by a border of tiny nodes. Together, the numerous teeth form a strong crushing surface. Single or associated teeth are quite commonly found in the Upper Cretaceous chalk of Europe.

Odontaspis (Carcharias)

Europe
Upper Cretaceous — Recent
Tooth height 1—4 cm

According to several texts the names *Odontaspis* and *Carcharias* are synonyms for the same genus, with the former being the name commonly used in popular literature. The genus has a cartilaginous skeleton and thus only the teeth are usually preserved after death. The teeth of *Odontaspis* are extremely common however, particularly in sands, sandstones, and phosphatic deposits. A typical tooth is high and sharply pointed, with a small subsidiary point present on either side and is usually brown or black in colour with a high gloss characterizing the tooth 'blade'. In sharks such as *Odontaspis*, the teeth grow in rows with continuous replacement of old and broken teeth.

Lepidotes

Europe, Africa, North America
Upper Triassic — Cretaceous
Individual scale length 2 cm

The genus *Lepidotes* is a bony fish of the holostean type. Today, the holosteans are represented by only two genera of North American freshwater fishes, the garpike *Lepidosteus* and the bowfin *Amia*. In general, holosteans such as *Lepidotes* are characterized by a 'symmetrical' tail and by a reduced number of stout unjointed fin bones. The holosteans were the characteristic ray-finned fishes of the Jurassic period. *Lepidotes* is a typical representative of this period with a rather heavily built structure and a short mouth lined with strong teeth. The scales of *Lepidotes* are thick and shiny with a diamond shape. *L. minor* from the Jurassic and *L. mantelli* from the Lower Cretaceous are representative species found fairly regularly in European localities.

Other Vertebrata
Trionyx (Turtles)

Europe, North America, Africa, Asia
Upper Cretaceous — Recent
Carapace plate width 3–10 cm

The remains of turtles are first known from rocks of Triassic age, with *Proganochelys* from Southern Germany being the oldest recorded genus. Triassic specimens are exceedingly rare however, and it is not until the Upper Jurassic that turtle bones become relatively common in sedimentary deposits. In the Upper Jurassic the genera *Pleurosternon* and *Plesiochelys* are well known in France and England, while in the Cretaceous, forms such as *Rhinochelys* (England) and *Allopleuron* (Holland) have limited distribution. Only in the Cainozoic are several genera common to many European countries, with *Trionyx*, a river turtle, being the most common of all. The most frequent remains of *Trionyx* are pieces of the carapace, usually the elongate costal bones, and the long bones of the limbs. The carapace of *Trionyx* is ornamented with a coarse reticulate pattern.

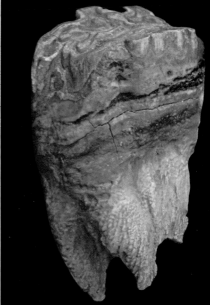

Deinotherium

Europe, Africa, Asia
Lower Miocene — Middle Pleistocene
Individual tooth width variable, 8–15 cm

Although related to *Mammut* within the Proboscidea (Elephants, Mammoths, Mastodons), *Deinotherium* is a rather strange animal. It represents a side branch in the family tree of the early elephant-like animals, having its tusks on the lower jaw. The tusks are rarely found as fossils in Europe but are characteristic in that they are curved sharply downwards and slightly backwards. The common fossils of *Deinotherium* are its teeth, with the cheek teeth being rather primitive and low crowned. Only the two back molars bear cross ridges similar to those of later genera. The animal's well-documented history suggests it disappeared in Europe and Asia during the Pliocene, but persisted in Africa during the Pleistocene. Species attributed to *Deinotherium* varied in size with early species attaining half the size of a recent elephant.

Equus

Europe, Americas, Africa, Asia
Pleistocene — Recent
Molar height 4—8 cm

Equus is the generic name given to the horse, donkey, and zebra which are the contemporary representatives of a long equid history. The first horses appeared almost 60 million years ago, with the small dog-sized *Hyracotherium* (*Eohippus*) roaming the forest glades of Europe and North America. With time, the horses increased in size and became plain dwellers, feeding on tough grasses and relying on speed as a defence against predators. Early horses from the Eocene, Oligocene, and Miocene exhibit a gradual change in skeletal structure with the teeth and limbs reflecting evolutionary modifications. In these horses the teeth were low crowned, while those of *Equus* are very high crowned with the upper crowns having a square outline and the lower crowns a rectangular one. Both upper and lower crowns have a complex pattern.

115

Mammut

Europe, North America, Africa, Asia
Miocene — Pleistocene
Tooth length variable, 12–17 cm

Since its remains are relatively common in the Pleistocene sediments of North America, *Mammut* is often referred to as the American mastodon. The teeth are among the most common remains and the large cheek teeth are particularly well known. They have several low cross-crests which by comparison are noticeably lower and more triangular than those of the elephantids. The enamel on the cheek teeth is very thick. Mastodons, like elephants, had large tusks on the upper jaw. They also had long flexible trunks and many grew to a large size. The last mastodons became extinct at the end of the Pleistocene. Many skeletons of *Mammut* have been discovered in postglacial swamps. It is interesting to think that these creatures roamed the earth only a few thousand years ago.

Birds

Worldwide
Jurassic — Recent
Variable size

The remains of fossil birds are uncommon, although spectacular discoveries such as those of *Archaeopteryx* from the Lithographic Stone of Bavaria (Jurassic) or of numerous isolated bones from the London Clay (Eocene) of England, do warrant particular merit. Bird bones are necessarily lightweight in construction and this does not aid in their preservation. They are usually best preserved in the low-energy environments of lakes or lagoons, where fine sediments settle to protect them. Fine mudstones and siltstones are fairly common in the Eocene of Europe and the discovery of feathers or limb bones, although rare, is a rewarding experience. The specimen illustrated was discovered recently at Menat in the Auvergne, France. It is the foot of an unnamed duck-like bird from sediments of Eocene age.

Trace Fossils

Trace fossils are the result of biological activity. They include tracks, trails, burrows, borings, and faecal deposits. Tracks and trails are the traces of active crawlers and are formed by their movement over the sea-floor (for example, due to migration or feeding). Burrows may reflect the need for a permanent home or for a temporary hiding or feeding place. Borings, however, are more permanent and it is likely that the remains of the animal that formed the structure will remain in situ. The geometry of the traces is controlled by the depositional environment in which the animal lives and therefore certain traces can be linked with a given habitat. It is possible, with the aid of trace fossils, for palaeontologists to reconstruct the environments that existed many millions of years ago. Trilobites and other arthropods are linked with the manufacture of many important traces.

Diplocraterion

Worldwide
Cambrian – Upper Jurassic and
    ? Recent
Tube diameter 2–4 cm
Distance between tubes 10–15 cm
Burrow depth 15–30 cm

The name *Diplocraterion* is given to vertical U-shaped burrows with **spreiten** (the lines indicating the former burrow position). In surface view the burrows appear as two equal openings which show an obvious pairing. In longitudinal section the burrow limbs are seen to be parallel without any obvious thickening. The 'U' is somewhat flattened and of equal diameter to the limbs. Spreiten are characteristic, occurring both above and below the base of the burrow. In forms where the spreiten occur between the limbs the indication is that the burrow is being extended downwards – protrusive; whereas burrows with spreiten below are migrating upwards – retrusive. This movement is in response to the rate of sedimentation and erosion. In *D. yoyo* the spreiten occur in both places.

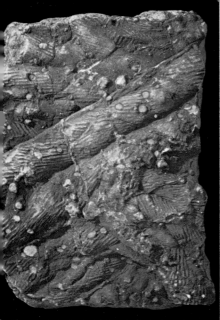

Cruziana

Worldwide
Cambrian – Silurian
Width 2–15 cm

In the study of trace fossils related species are referred to an **ichnogenus**, with the name *Cruziana* being used in the association of tracks made by trilobites and trilobite-like arthropods. The tracks consist of two lobes which are the result of the scratchings of the walking part (telopodite) of the branched limb. In some cases, the traces are long and the lobes parallel, while others are short and almost heart-shaped. These represent the behaviour of the animal, with the long furrows suggesting direct travel and the short type representing resting burrows. Over thirty species have been recognized and some like *C. furcifera* and *C. semiplicata* are used for stratigraphic purposes.

Arenicolites

Europe, North America
Cambrian – Recent
Tube diameter 2–5 mm

The name *Arenicolites* is used with reference to U-shaped burrows of various dimensions. They are vertical to the sea-floor and have rounded openings. Unlike traces such as *Diplocraterion yoyo* from the Jurassic, *Arenicolites* lacks any evidence of burrowing either between the descending tubes or below the curve of the burrow. The evidence in question takes the form of curved lines that reflect the former position of the burrow; the lines are called **spreiten**. In comparison with *Diplocraterion* and *Rhizocorallium* (an oblique to horizontal trace particularly abundant in Jurassic sediments) *Arenicolites* has a simple structure although a few species have sculptured or lined walls. It is unlikely that all the traces referred to the ichnogenus *Arenicolites* were created by the same animal genus.

Thalassinoides

Europe, Asia
Triassic — Tertiary
Width 2—5 cm

The name *Thalassinoides* was first used
to describe ramifying cylindrical burrows from the Miocene. These burrows
were horizontal with repeated Y-
shaped branching and slight swellings
at the forks. Since that time, thalassinoid traces have been discovered in
sediments of Mesozoic age and com-
parable structures have been noted
from Tertiary sediments. The discovery
of arthropod droppings and scratch
marks in some fossil burrows clearly
indicates the type of animal that made
the trace; with the crab *Callianassa*
being directly associated by some
authorities. Thalassinoid burrows are
very common in Jurassic and Cretaceous sediments, where small
burrows tend to indicate low-energy
conditions and large burrows indicate
high-energy environments.

Coprolites

Worldwide
Palaeozoic — Recent
Size variable

Coprolites and faecal pellets are the fossilized droppings of the waste material
of animals. To some extent the use of
either name depends on the size of the
pellet or dropping, with microcoprolite
and faecal pellet being synonymous.
Coprolites are of moderate to large
size with the droppings of Cretaceous
reptiles or Cainozoic mammals pro-
viding good examples; specimens of
30—35 cm have been recorded. Many
coprolites are rounded featureless
structures, while others are spirally
coiled. Faecal pellets are usually less
than 0·5 cm in length and may represent the waste materials of invertebrates including fish. In some localities,
faecal pellets are abundant in burrows
formerly occupied by gastropods. Coprolites and faecal pellets should not
be confused with the 'gizzard stones'
of some reptiles.

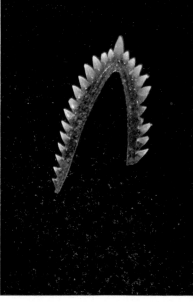

Serpula

Europe, North America
Silurian — Recent
Length 2–5 cm

The calcareous tubes of *Serpula* are deposited by polychaete worms. They are round, angular, or slightly flattened in section. Some are long and straight while others are irregularly curved or spirally coiled. The thickness of the calcareous wall is variable but the majority can be described as robust. Polychaete worms are gregarious animals and their tubes are often found in closely packed clusters or raised mounds. Many tubes have a smooth surface but others, such as *S. limax* from the Jurassic of France, have a distinct ornament of transverse striations and longitudinal ridges. Serpulid masses are common to both ancient and modern-day shallow-water environments.

Conodont

Worldwide
Ordovician — Triassic
Width 0·5–2 mm

Conodonts are small tooth- or plate-like fossils found essentially in rocks of the Palaeozoic era. Their origin is uncertain, although at times they have been associated with gastropods, worms, and fish among others. Conodonts are composed of calcium phosphate and are usually discovered by the chemical solution of limestones. The vast majority have a brown to black colouration, and they usually have a glassy appearance but may be either fibrous or layered in structure. Genera such as *Palmatolepis* and *Polygnathus* are well-known genera from the Devonian. These and other conodont genera are useful in the stratigraphic subdivision of Palaeozoic rocks. As with other microfossils they are of particular interest to oil geologists.

Plants

Fossil plants have been recorded from rocks over 3000 million years old. They were simple filament-like organisms belonging to the blue-green algae. The simple algae prevailed until vascular plants migrated into terrestrial niches during the Silurian. At first, land plants were also rather simple, the psilophytopsids of the Silurian and Devonian lacking true roots or leaves. During the late Devonian and Carboniferous the lycopsid, sphenopsid, and early fern-like plants appeared and formed the major component of coal-measure floras. In late Palaeozoic times these plants were replaced by the conifers and cycads which prevailed until the expansion of the true flowering plants (angiosperms) in the early Cretaceous. By the Upper Cretaceous the oak, beech, magnolia, willow, and plane were well represented in various floras. Fossil plants are useful indicators of palaeoclimates, and spores and pollen are important in the dating of strata.

Chara

Worldwide
Triassic — Recent
Length up to 1 mm

Chara is a member of one of the simplest plant groups, namely the algae. Together with other genera it forms the order Charales, which represent a distinct evolutionary line away from all other green algae. The method of reproduction within the group is sexual, and in *Chara*, well-developed male and female organs called **antheridia** and **oogonia** respectively, are developed. *Chara* and a few other genera secrete calcium carbonate and the oogonia often possess a calcareous envelope. In fact, all fossil charaphytes are almost exclusively known from calcified oogonia. The oogonia are composed of a limited number of cells which are arranged in a right- or left-handed spiral around a central cavity, which in life contains the oospore. The calcium carbonate is secreted internally and may adopt the cell form to give a ridged and furrowed appearance.

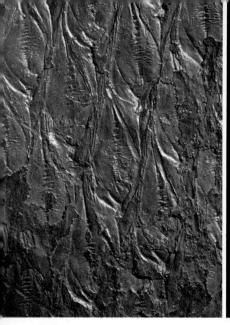

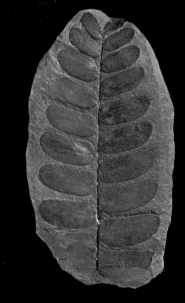

Lepidodendron

Europe
Carboniferous
Fragment size variable

Lepidodendron is one of the best known of all coal-measure plants. It is a member of the Lycopsida or club mosses, but unlike the small, herbaceous genera of today, it was a giant among early plants; with individual 'trees' attaining a height of 40–50 m. *Lepidodendron* and related genera such as *Sigillaria*, are often called scale trees due to the presence of closely packed leaf scars over the stem surface. In *Lepidodendron* the leaf scars, which indicate the former position of the small leaves, have a rounded diamond shape and a spiral arrangement. During life the tree, like modern counterparts, possessed a stem, root, and spore bodies, but due to geological processes these are rarely found together and different names have been used in their description. For example, *Lepidostrobus* is the name given to the 'cones' of *Lepidodendron*.

Neuropteris

Europe, North America, Asia,
   North Africa, China
Carboniferous — Permian
Leaflet length 1–3 cm

Neuropteris is a member of an important order of seed-bearing vascular plants called the Pteridospermae. Many of these plants resemble the ferns, having large multipinnate leaves and a characteristic venation. The fern-like fronds of *Neuropteris* are very common in Carboniferous coal measure deposits, often being found in association with fronds of the genus *Alethopteris*. In *Neuropteris*, the pinnules are rounded distally and offset along the leaf stem. On the inner edge the pinnules appear broad and somewhat lobed, curving gently away from the midline vein. The venation is simple. The form of the pinnules differs considerably from those of *Alethopteris* which are slimmer, straighter, and fused with the leaf stem.

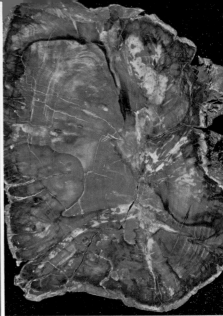

Calamites

Asia, Europe, North America
Carboniferous — Lower Permian
Fragment size variable

The remains of the jointed stems of plants such as *Calamites* are common in sediments of the Carboniferous coal measures. The structure of *Calamites* and related genera closely resembles that of the living genus, *Equisetum* the horsetail plant. Unlike *Equisetum* however, which rarely exceeds 30 cm in height, the stems of *Calamites* can exceed 30 cm in width and attain a height of some 30 m. *Calamites* is usually preserved as compressions and casts with a surface of carbonaceous material. As stated, the stem is jointed with the external surface having a ribbed appearance. In some fossils, it is possible to recognize leaf-bearing nodes and branch scars. A thin section of Calamites would, under a microscope, show a pith layer, protoxylem, and a distinct cortical layer.

Fossil Wood

Worldwide
Carboniferous — Recent
Size variable

The remains of tree stems, roots, and branches have been deposited in lake and inshore sediments since late Palaeozoic times. Huge sections of scale trees are found in coal measure deposits while the wood and cones of pines are common in many post Jurassic localities. In the late Cretaceous, the angiosperms became the dominant plant group and fossil wood from trees such as the oak (*Quercus*) and the palm (*Palmoxylon*) is common. Fossil woods are often preserved in arid environments, where the tissues of the plant become impregnated with silica. Sections through wood preserved in this way reveal the growth rings and arrangement of vascular bundles. In *Quercus*, a dicotyledon, the vascular bundles are confined to the outer section of the stem, while in the monocotyledon, *Palmoxylon*, they are scattered at random and growth rings do not develop.

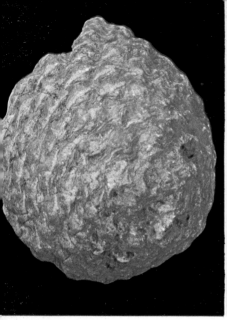

Conifers

Worldwide
Upper Carboniferous — Recent
Cone size 5–10 cm

The conifers comprise one of the most important groups of trees, which includes the pines and redwoods and are characterized by their seeds being borne in cones. Although the earliest pines are recorded from the Upper Palaeozoic, they did not really dominate floras until Triassic to Jurassic times. The conifers are woody branching plants in which the leaves are usually needle- or scale-like with a whorled or spiral arrangement. Wood and cones are the most common fossilized remains of conifers, with excellent cones being recorded from many Cretaceous localities. The cone pictured above, belongs to taxodiaceous conifers which, today, are represented by the giant redwoods and by genera such as *Taxodium* in the fossil record. The once important *Taxodium* is now confined to North America and Guatemala.

Ginkgo

Worldwide
Permian — Recent
Leaf lobe length 2–3 cm

The ginkgo tree is an example of a living fossil and the last representative of a group of plants that can probably be traced back to the Upper Palaeozoic. *Ginkgo* is a gymnosperm, the wood of which is very similar to that of the gymnosperm conifers. The gymnosperms are known as the 'naked seed' plants, and they lack the conspicuous vessels and ray structures of most dicotyledonous flowering plants. *Ginkgo* is noted for the character of its leaves which are clustered at the end of short branches. The form of the individual leaf varies throughout the ages, with the early Mesozoic forms being divided into narrow blades. Later forms are broader with deeply cut lobes and parallel veins. *G. biloba* is the only living species, found especially in China and North America.

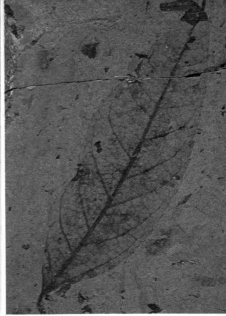

Nipa

Europe, Malaysia
Lower Eocene — Recent
Seed length 5–15 cm

Nipa is an angiosperm of the monocotyledon type. It is a palm, characterized by having large fruits and a stem
which, in cross-section, shows the
vascular bundles to be scattered.
Today, the grasses are the most common representatives of the monocotyledons, but in the past this position
was held by the palms. Fossil palms
are important constituents of post-
Jurassic floras and are used by
palaeontologists as indicators of
palaeoclimates. *Nipa* is particularly
well known through the discovery of
its large subtriangular fruits in the
Eocene of Europe and its pollen in the
Lower Eocene of Borneo, and through
to its occurrence in Malaysia today.
Its presence in these two areas at
different times, indicates that a tropical
climate once prevailed in what is now
a temperate region.

Laurus

Worldwide
Cretaceous — Recent
Leaf length 8–12 cm

The leaf of the genus *Laurus*, the laurel,
is selected as a representative of the
angiosperms. These form the most
important group of living plants, the
first representatives of which appeared
in the Cretaceous period. Angiosperms
are also known as the flowering plants
and are divided into two stocks, the
dicotyledons and monocotyledons.
These stocks are characterized by the
structure of their seeds, vascular tissue,
and leaf venation. In dicotyledons such
as *Laurus*, the young seed plant has
two cotyledons for food storage and
the leaf has a complex network of
veins. The monocotyledons, however,
such as *Acer* (sycamore) has a single
cotyledon and parallel venation in the
leaf. The leaf of *Laurus* has an entire
margin and secondary veins arise from
a main midline vein.

Index